NOT WITHOUT MY HIJAB

11 STEPS TO RECLAIMING YOUR FAITH

By Halimah Deoliveira

First edition published
December 2017

For information regarding bulk purchases of this book, digital purchase and
special discounts, please contact the author at

ISBN-13: 978-1793493859
ISBN-10: 1793493855

www.beyouinhd.com

halimah@beyouinhd.com

For Upcoming Stageplay cities
Email info@beyouinhd.com

بِسْمِ اللَّهِ الرَّحْمَٰنِ الرَّحِيمِ

"In the name of God, most Gracious, most Compassionate

This book was written only by the permission of Allah and I'm prayerful that it will be of benefit to the reader. This book is dedicated to my Grandma Edna, Grandpa Melvin, Grandma Esther, my children Isaiah and Jennah (everything I do is for you). I want to express extreme gratitude to my mother and father and ask God to bestow His highest blessings on them. Thank you to a host of family and friends who gave me the courage to write this book Sonia, Tmiela, Lorell, Andrylyn, Nehemiah, Travis and Jibreel you all rock!

Authors Note:

Dear Reader:

A small confession, I almost didn't write this book. I wasn't sure if I was ready to share my story. If the world was ready. If I had earned the right to tell the story to the world just yet. Then I decided that God would not have placed the desire and the strong urge to share my truth if it wasn't the right time to share. Releasing the kid version of this book, "Jennah's First Hijab" empowering Muslim children to tackle the issue of hijab being a choice and how to develop a strong foundation in their identity, helped give me the courage to write this book. Through the writing of my first book "Jennah's First Hijab" I was able to reach the mothers of the next generation of believers and inheritors of the earth. I found that we shared similar stories and then I knew the time was "NOW" to write and release this book. While I wrote the latter as a prevention tool for the children, before they become the confused, defeated adults, we are today. Many women are suffering in silence because they feel they are alone in their struggle with finding a solid religious foundation, feel shame for not having enough faith, for not having a relationship with God by way of a religion that seems so rigid in its handling of those who struggle with their faith. Of the innumerable number of world religions, Islam can easily be identified as the least desirable if you want to be free, cool or hip.

Embarrassed to share my childhood traumas and not wanting to taint the religion I so love has held me back from telling the whole story. My religious beliefs that one Muslim covers the sins of another Muslim is another factor. So, I'm not telling the story to uncover sins, to ridicule, bring shame or seek validation.

I am writing it however to help women who feel they have gone too far down a one-way street to be able to turn around and reclaim their faith.

In my travels I've encountered, many women appear to suffer with the misconception to be successful in business or accepted in society they have to diminish or denounce their faith or beliefs in "Not Without My Hijab". Despite the adversity I faced while navigating College, Corporate America and relationships I was relentlessly determined to succeed. Embattled in hardship, setbacks, race, gender and religious discrimination, I developed 11 Steps to Reclaiming Your Faith a guaranteed system to ensure your victory. How do I know the steps work? They are the very steps I used to find my way back!

UNVEILING

Daylight, for the life of me I'll never be able to tell you why I picked this vacation and this day to start taking up new hobbies. Particularly one that involves a motorcycle. I booked a trip to Italy and had promised myself I would try something new. You know scratch something off the bucket list. I had ridden on the back of a motorcycle one time before, on a trip to D.R. but I was 18 then. Now at 39 and just 6 months shy of my 40th birthday I wasn't sure this was a good idea.

I was winding down the streets in Naples without a helmet!!! I could kick myself for:

1- Writing this on my bucket list

2- For thinking this was a good idea and

3- For letting my friend talk me into it after I had already said “No”.

With age comes wisdom and I should have known better when I saw the route winding down a narrow cobblestone street that this was going to be a disaster. God, if I survive this I promise I'll do everything you've asked of me, I'll write that book (this one), open a women's shelter and feed the homeless every week on Thursday instead of just twice a month as originally planned. God? God? God? I know you hear me. Now you want to know the worst part, I'm actually starting to enjoy the ride.

Oh, how I so wanted this to be the introduction to this book and story which is why I didn't leave it out. Functioning as an un-manifested affirmation of sorts. I will look back on this years from now after many trips to Italy and say "I saw it before I saw it "and the plan is to make it manifest in this year of 40. Pre-writing it as Chapter 1 in March 2017 is a testament to my determination, when I first started writing this book. An elaborate plan that by May 1st I would have been on my way to Italy. Placing the deposit with a travel agent, is usually a sign that a trip for me is a go. Space was left below to insert the questions and later insert the details.

WHAT ARE YOU ENJOYING IN ITALY (INSERT LATER)

HOW ARE THE PEOPLE? (INSERT HERE)

WHAT DOES IT LOOK LIKE THERE? (INSERT HERE)

WHAT DOES IT SMELL LIKE? (A "foodie" question INSERT HERE)

Happy to report, God had another course for me, some of you may be disappointed that this is not how this story begins, don't fret it will come true one day soon and my sole mission will be to take every selfie under the beautiful sun in a gorgeous, bright yellow hijab. Capture that scene on a white moped, galivanting down the middle of a narrow cobblestone street in the heart of Italy! Ok?

God has lead me down a road that is just as wild and adventurous and unpredictable as winding down that bumpy cobblestone street in some faraway place will be for me. He knows me better, he knew that that trip would have been a distraction from doing the internal work necessary to get this book written the way it needed to be written and to take hold of my life. This book is a compilation of my personal experiences with religion throughout my 39 plus years on this planet and an affirmation that the next 40 will be devoted to God and the "Life Plan" he has destined for me.

My undying prayer is to give hope to the girl or now woman reading this book that has experienced a broken heart in childhood, people falling off shelves and shattering, people that never came to the rescue and being the girl with no real hope of escaping the shackles of her past, this is my tribute to her, my promise that through patience and prayer you will be free. Summon the most amazing force in the universe Ash Shaafi, (The Healer), Al-Mu'id (The Restorer) and Ar-Razzaq (The Bestower of Sustenance) just 3 of Allah's 99 beautiful names.

Despite my pulp fictionesque intro I don't want to give

the whole story away up front. Another shameless share about myself, (FYI: I left nothing out, the book is filled with shameless shares) for as long as I can remember I've run away from God with vigor and haste. Arrogantly forgetting that God's tracking system would inevitably find me wherever I go. In every aspect of my life, I've let go of relationships, jobs, homes when things were too Godly or comfortable. Alife of ease was a foreign concept before the A.P.P.L.I.C.A.T.I.O.N. of the 11 steps.

I'm sure you want to know a little about me "How did I get here?"

I was born to two amazing parents on what my mother describes as the best day and reason to give up her thanksgiving dinner. She tells this story often when asked about my birth. the hospital distributed the Thanksgiving issue meals and my mother ate her portion. To which I responded, "No thank you", she sacrificed her meal, (vomit everywhere, gross I know) born naturally just under a month earlier, an event that would repeat itself 29 years later with the birth of my own daughter. I came as a welcome surprise to say the least, as fortune would have it they did not give her a new meal after my arrival. This early arrival and hastiness would follow me as a theme throughout the rest of my life. 7lbs and some odd ounces bundle of hair, almond eyes and caramel completed skin. My memories of this time in my life are only realized through photographs, ones of my older brother and I playing on the floor in our Brooklyn apartment, with a beautiful white fireplace in the background(this place I've seen in my dreams many times, it is my safe place) and having a Fisher Price phone (complete with red handle and long cord, spin dial and made of indestructible material to boot) that I played with until I was much older and surely passed down to a sibling or two.

Events surrounding my father's sudden death are untraceable in my memory bank, although his absence was undeniably felt. Holding onto this idea that if my daddy were here many things I've gone through would not have happened, then again, I probably wouldn't have written this book or be talking to you. True greatness and strength is born out of tragedy and despair, you cannot claim to know one without knowing the other. It is the seemingly calamitous events in our lives that we want to forget that make us unique and powerful contributors.

Daddy passing was the first time I experienced loss and disappointment. Everyone who knew me then knew how much I adored him. I don't have a single picture with him, no tangible keepsake to say, "I belonged to him". Withheld from a "Bereavement Experience" for my father both delayed and aggravated the symptoms. Undergoing this considerable tribulation would have taught me coping skills around loss, achieving intimacy and closeness in my relationships, instead I struggle to express these characteristics with people I'm close to. Indubitably an area in my remedial life class that I'm still improving on and developing. Holding firm to faith and letting go of characteristics that only my creator possesses, has helped me in this area.

Beholden to God for the memories real or imagined that are either trapped in the recesses of my mind and I've managed to tap into or the ones that I've conjured up to console myself. A part of me still grieves for him, I pray for him every day even so, I no longer wonder "What if?" while clinging to those fantasies of being "daddy's girl", those aren't the cards I was dealt. Dedicating my life to giving and telling my story, is my legacy, the give back so my neglected childhood will not be in vain.

This is not a movie, and I'm not "Wonder Woman", this is real life, a true story, my story that has the power to change lives, lift the spirits of women globally, diminish the confusion, sorrow and anger I know injured parties feel. "Everything will be ok", coming from a child who has experienced death at a young age, my advice to parents and guardians is it is extremely important that you give the child the opportunity to grieve, let them know it's not their fault and sign them up for therapy even if you think they don't need it.

Remembrance is a wonderfully mysterious thing.

Kudos to the Doctors, Psychiatrists, Psychologists and other Mental Health Professionals who spend their time refining their craft to help people like me tap into what is trapped in the mind. I could only write this book once I was able to confront, recall and assemble them chronologically.

Each of us is responsible for our own healing (present tense because this is a journey and there are more situations we may encounter in the future that will bring up past hurts.) How you deal with them will determine how you'll move forward. Affirm, I am 100% responsible for how I feel, 100% responsible for the energy I give off and therefore 100% responsible for who and what I allow into my space. Adherence to my faith was paramount to me overcoming these situations. Connecting to God, gives me a path to how I can connect with myself.

Grateful to my parents for bringing me into this world and for my mother especially instilling values, morals and just being the epitome of what it means to be a survivor. Teaching us. To seek God first and not rely on your own understanding. She fixated on the bright side of life no matter what was going on showing us a brave face even when she was falling apart herself. I'm reminded of the term "Smile it's sunnah" (Sunnah is the way of Prophet Muhammad S.A.W.) when I think of all we endured in that 12 years. Alhamdullillah (All praises due to God) for giving us a way out and allowing us to endure and then overcome.

Slow Poison

Ignorance costs! Not a complete sentence but it is a complete thought. We weren't allowed to attend my father's funeral because my mother was told that religiously speaking "Women cannot follow funeral processions." at the time of his death my mother and father were both "New" converts to Islam. Both adopted being "5 percenters", then (NOI) Nation of Islam (only my father) and later accepted Islam. Attending the funeral may have given me complete closure and the chance to say, "See you later".

Thirty years later, I became aware of where my father was buried on the day of my paternal grandmother's funeral. Crying uncontrollably that day in the limo, at the grave site and for days later, so angry at the fact that there was no grave marker with his name on it!! Searching for someone to blame, someone to feel the pain of his loss, a grieving partner, validation and a parting "goodbye". The funeral afforded the ability to enact what would have possibly played out when he passed. Seeking tangible evidence that he lived, he was here, no matter how small he made an impact on the world, there was a little girl that loved him. No one shared in my sentiment, they had already come to terms with the loss 30 years prior and were mourning the loss of my grandmother, I was left mourning them both.

His loss was an unwelcome, POISON, that I gradually

internalized forming a “cancer” around my heart. The cancer grew larger, from every internalization of events, instead of praying and entrusting them to God, I held onto them afraid to let go, that I would let go of the memories, that it somehow meant I approved of the offenses in my life.

Shortly after my father died my mother remarried, for fear of having fatherless, orphaned children so she prayed for a husband. One with knowledge to instill a strong religious foundation and financial soundness to travel the world. She prayed for shallow characteristics as she tells the story now. Inadvertently leaving out seemingly minute details like loving stepfather, patient, kind and gentle husband. Nevertheless, he was studying Islamic Studies (religious knowledge, check) and living abroad in Medina, Saudi Arabia (world travel, check).

Pictures of my older brother and I donning matching royal blue jackets with a yellow stripe on the shoulder, and the same dazed and confused looks on our faces it’s fuzzy for my mom but from the stories I remember, everything happened pretty quickly and I'm sure our faces in the photo captured at the airport the day we left, mirrored the chaos and uncertainty around us.

Our first few months were vague; my brother and I often reminisce about playing in the empty lot next door. Empty with the exception of the debris from a building that once stood in the spot where this mountainous mass of broken bricks and shards of metal now stood, next to the 3-story building where we lived. Habitually getting in trouble for coming back with soiled clothes, we undoubtedly experienced our first series of cuts and bruises in that lot.

Medina produced many noteworthy memories, one of them being the times we played with the neighbor kid, Hatim and trips across the roadway to another neighbor's house who had goats on the roof. What Medina story would be complete without recalling the different animals you encounter in the city? Especially one of a goat eating a can straight out of the garbage and being so amazed that no one stopped him from doing this!!! (we later discovered that the goats never swallowed the cans they were just curiously determining if the can was edible or not)

The city was so beautiful, extremely hot during the day a dry heat, no humidity meaning your clothes didn't stick to you. My love for the sun was birthed during our time here, the presence of the sun meant I was outdoors, alive and free. Followed by cool nights crisp, clean air and little noise or movement.

Prayer at the masjid was my favorite time, it was within walking distance and you could see the green light emitting from the tower from any direction. When the adhan (Islamic call to prayer) sounded it sent a peace over me that I still feel today anytime I hear it. Most days we walked the distance for prayer at the mosque, sadness always fell over me when we couldn't go. Even at 3 and 4 years old I felt a deep connection to God, and enjoyed performing prayer I was always at peace during the process. There was this connection to God I felt, and talking to him always brought clarity and the ability to go on.

It wasn't long before we were injected with more poison, toxic actions and displays of love. We were introduced to what I now know was Domestic Violence, I remember being frightened at first and then it being routine, so we assumed our positions and played in the workout room. Which was usually where they stuck us until the fight or altercation was over, or it was prayer time, tea time or time to eat. Most of my memories of this time in our life were of being in the workout room, going to the mosque and playing on the asbestos mountain, a joke we would later make that playing on that hill of debris was probably not the best idea. Going to and from the mosques, travelling to Jeddah and all the other places in between (including the time we were at the bank of the Red Sea trying to catch frogs at night) cultivated my adventurous spirit and desire to travel. The most memorable of those places was the Marketplace, an open space where vendors sold their goods everything from rice, to abayas, to fruit to books. Of the many faces and characters, the one that will always standout was the beggar woman, she wore a black abaya and she crawled around the Marketplace. Missing a foot and a hand which is why she crawled instead of walked around. My brother and I looked for her every trip, staring as if to ask my mother "What's her deal?" and amazed how despite the incapacitation she managed just fine. My mother later answered our inquisitive looks by explaining that her missing hand and foot was the consequence for stealing, taking something that did not belong to her and she had been caught twice.

Why didn't she learn her lesson the first time? Such a naive thought, I'm sure some people could say that about my life, why hadn't I come back to the religion I love sooner? When deep down inside I always knew I was going to return. Perhaps for the same reason that she went back and stole again, she knew that what she was doing was not right but maybe it was what she needed to do to survive that day. Maybe she wasn't strong enough to do the work she would need to do to get the job she needed to be able to afford what she stole versus stealing it. The lesson she left me with is that God's mercy surpasses His wrath, He may bring you a temporary punishment in hopes that it will cure you not to harm you but to cure you. God could have put in the judges head to cut off her other hand when she stole again but he didn't he showed mercy and chose her foot instead. Leaving her with one of her hands to make it easy.

More Poison or Infusion of Faith

By this time the very thing my mother didn't want for us, the feeling like outsiders, not being a part of a family had happened anyway. We were made to feel inadequate at every opportunity. My mother had given birth to my younger brother and sister and that solidified his family that we were not welcome to be a part of. We were our mother's children but not his. I was never his daughter I was always Halimah his stepdaughter. There was always this inner struggle being one way and saying things his way when he was around and then being normal when he wasn't around. Trying to be the way he wanted you to be, not because you cared or wanted to but to stay below the radar, so he wouldn't start in on you or anyone else for that matter.

My mother always made the effort to console and uplift my brother and I after he had belittled us. I even have a lump in my throat as I write this. Feeling less than and inadequate does something to the human spirit, constantly working to live up to an unrealistic expectation. More poison, it was routine now, second nature, I knew who I had to be when he was around and waited until he was gone so I could be myself. I relied heavily on my brother at this time, he somehow managed to escape his rants so I would follow his lead. My mother who was usually in the line of fire, had no control or say in the situation, after experiencing domestic violence as an adult, I now know she was fighting for her life, just like we were.

Finding the way out was long and hard, my mother stayed married to him for 12 years and the mental conditioning only continued and escalated. We had some eventful things happen in the middle, there are some bright spots but honestly my childhood is an area of pain for me. It's a reminder of a time where I had no control over what was happening to me. There were generous strangers along the way who gave me just enough hope to keep me going. Looking back my faith started to dissipate, I started losing my connection to God the longer we stayed, the further the distance.

Back in the U.S., and 2 more siblings (my 2 baby sisters) there was a little more freedom meaning the hours where we didn't have to be in his presence for 9-10 months were longer. School, I dove into school it was the one thing in my life I could control I could live, thrive and flourish here. He couldn't tell me to fail here, he couldn't diminish me here. I owned this part of my life. When there was a snow day I was hurt and disappointed, it meant we would be in the house with him.

The physical and mental abuse continued, at age 6 I was, sexually molested. The first time, I was very afraid and instinctively knew it was wrong but told not to tell.

Confused and hurt that it was happening to me, I went into a shell of myself (a child who is the victim of domestic violence is likely to experience some type of sexual assault as well) effects of this still show up in my present day, the smell of stove top popcorn popping triggers these memories. After therapy, (yes, I'm an advocate) I let the memories come, give myself permission to feel whatever emotion comes, then immediately go into gratitude to God.

Some may think of me as strange, but I'm not thankful these things happened to me, I'm thankful for what they taught me. Religiously speaking I now know, that each trauma was the qadr ("the divine decree and the predestination") of Allah. Not some grave punishment for sins, I was 2, what sins could I have possibly committed at 2, 3 and 6?

I rarely spoke about my secret whether inside or outside the home. I kept my story to myself. Happy, loud and boisterous at school, the total opposite of who I was at home. The conditioning and reinforcement to not tell continued. So much so that I didn't even tell my best friend (My maternal grandmother) when she blatantly asked me when I was 14, I just jumped ahead, let me go back a bit.

At 12, one of my siblings belted out that I was being molested. My mother immediately approached the guilty party who vehemently denied the allegations, she then asked my friends at school "what they were putting me up to?" They had no idea what she was talking about, *I had never told them*. I stood frozen as she continued her inquest, thankful when it was over that she hadn't divulged too much information that I could easily explain away. In school I made up stories about how wonderful my home life was, it made it easier to cope with what was going on at home. Two more years we all endured more of the same and we all did extremely well in school never missed a day despite the horror we endured after school. I was grateful for "the inquest" because it reduced the number of times I encountered my transgressor. Prayers answered.

Finally, the escape plan, we started taking bags of clothes to my grandparents' house every week we went for quranic studies, this went on for months, so we wouldn't have much to pack on the day we left. The final straw for my mother was when she would find knives under our pillows at night. The final week, he was on edge worse than usual I want to say it was a Friday and that meant we would be around him all weekend in this mood. He had ripped the phone cord out of the wall a couple of times that week which meant "no phone calls". What he didn't know was my mother had a hidden one she had bought, this was a routine, we all knew where it was, and played timekeeper for my mom whenever she was on the phone. Sneaking outside was another part of this game and our opportunity at having a childhood. We played on the roof, just below my brother's bedroom window or ran to the park, where my younger siblings played on the swings and enjoyed jumping rope. Despite the short visits to the park my two brothers and I had become experts at handball and paddleball. (The parks brother/sister unbeatable Dynamic Duo)

Making it home by climbing to the roof at the end of the block and making it down the roof hatch and home in time, to wash up and pretend to be miserable before he came home. As we waited to see what type of mood he came home in, I remember a heaviness coming over me, this inner strength and resolve that I would not endure another day of him terrorizing me or anyone else.

Thinking about the possibilities of the weekend, I took the short trip from my room, past the bathroom to the kitchen and retrieved "The Cleaver", not sure what I was about to do I just remember thinking and feeling that I had enough and "Not Today". I stood at the crevice of the doorway, my small frame hidden and practicing my aim with "The Cleaver".

Heavy footsteps approaching, stomach and teeth clenching I knew it was "On" by the way he was walking up the steps. Practicing the mechanics, I slid "The Cleaver" out from its case, carefully placing it back into its cover. My respect for my mother's instructions on how to care for the kitchen utensil, to always place it back in the holster, clean it once it was used, is what would give me away. The scene, our small one bedroom, Brooklyn railroad flat apartment, as they called them, with the entrance at the center of all the rooms you could see me at my perch no matter where you were standing in the house.

Before he reached the top of the landing and opened the front door my mother screamed out "No" which alerted my brother who came and held my arm back with "The Cleave" simultaneously my mother dialed my grandmother, told her to come get us and bring the cops. By that time, he had entered the house to this scene and he immediately knew something was wrong. He ripped the phone cord out of the wall, "predictable" and started in, what happened next is fuzzy. The most gratifying moment was walking out the door, past the sight of him on his knees facing out the window in my brother's room which was really the dining room. His reign was over, the tyrant had lost.

I never looked back wanting that experience wanting anything that had to do with that part of my life. I wanted to be done with it. Couldn't wait to start a new school and just be anywhere but back there. I have ridden past the address on sunny Atlantic Ave, in Brooklyn many times and I have always smiled only ever wanting to remember the day I left. As I'm writing this, I am grateful for everything in between, that everything in between would guide me back to Reclaiming my Faith. My undesirable past offering a window into what life used to be like, where I've been and where I could go back to, not physically but emotionally and spiritually offer up the reason for staying the path.

STEP 1:

AWAKEN

In choosing to write this book I truly wanted to capture what it was like for me to Awaken and start the road to reclaiming my faith, in hopes that more people would be able to do the same. This has not been an easy process for me and please trust that I am still growing into my "Faith walk" learning and evolving more and more every day. The *Spiritual Awakening* that happens is crucial to the process hence why I have included it as the first step. I thought that I was ready for this step many times over the last 20 years and I'll be honest I have given it what I consider a valiant effort each time. Some of these attempts lasted as short as an afternoon and others as long as a week.

The one that was for an afternoon was an emotional attempt I was so angry at my spouse that I was doing and saying things out of spite. I had no true intentions of actually following through with it because honestly, I wasn't ready to face myself and do the work. The most recent attempt before these last 3 years was the Spring before my last attempt. I looked for all the beautifully colored scarves of every texture in my closet that were long enough to wrap my head and I prepared them for the week, along with the most modest clothes I could find. Even my son wasn't hopeful. He said, "How long is this one going to last mom?" As sure as he was about his statement was as sure as within a week I had gone back to my regular routine. Which included weekends with my friends, beach trips, restaurants, vacations, yoga class and work. None of those activities incorporated the remembrance of God or anything external to myself. I operated as the creator of my universe and everything in it. Religion and the concept of anything outside of myself as having power or control over me had become a foreign concept over these last 20 years. I never denounced my faith, but I never claimed it either.

If you haven't gathered as of yet I am a Muslim woman, a believer in the religion Islam. So not covering in hijab or khimar (the religious covering prescribed for women in Islam in the Holy Quran 24:30-31) or praying (Quran 2:43-2:45) are both considered to be a huge sin. The only reason I tell my story is not to expose my sin but to offer a glimpse as to what can happen if you go too long without connecting to source, "God" and to deter or diminish the amount of time religious women spend away from communicating to God.

My prayer is that my awakening helps strengthen, encourage and empower you to have your own. I truly believe I walked around with "Blinders" on as to God's magnificence and everything amazing He has created both in nature and in the human spirit. I am amazed by how he used my tragedies to lead me to my triumphs, how merciful God has been to someone who not only did not acknowledge His presence but also walked around angry and resentful at all the terrible things He seemingly allowed me to go through. I now know that those things happened for me and not to me! God was calling me, nudging me in hopes that each tragic episode would bring me closer to Him.

He even used my beloved father to connect with me in dreams. Anytime I was in a relationship or situation too deep and one that would have sent me down the road of no return, my father came to me in a dream. I welcomed his beautiful face, I always knew it was him, he was dressed in white and he would come to me and give me advice and then he would leave which was always followed by me experiencing this free fall in my dreams (Falling in dreams is an indication of insecurity, instability and anxiety it is also attributed to marriage failures , changing of spouse, profession, country or religion) Girl let me tell you God sent my "Daddy" to get me out of all of the above. I love Him for that, for rescuing me from myself!

A chance meeting with a wise older woman, we'll call "Ann" would help me understand these dreams and just how God works happened earlier this year, volunteering at a girls' detention center here in

Philadelphia. I don't know why but I told her everything about me including about these stories and dreams. And the advice she offered was amazing, I was so angry with God, running from him at every turn not wanting to talk to him, not wanting anything to do with him. Trying to find protectors, consolers in other people, He knew coming to me as HIMSELF, was going to be met with resistance. Instead He used a welcoming, median my father.

Proudly telling people my father came to me in dreams, as my hero and saviour from poor decisions, relationships and/or jobs. Ironically the symbolic revelations from my father ended when I began the journey back to Islam. I instinctively knew I wouldn't see him again, The Father of All mankind including my own father had connected with me, my heart and soul. Experiencing the brink of all the loss it needed to finally tip and say, "I've had enough, I get it, I see you, I see you" I remember crying uncontrollably on my knees in the shower, of my bright yellow master bathroom saying "Enough".

My life shifts centered around my global travel, I divorced my husband after ten years of marriage, we weren't equally yoked. I favored Islam and his faith had dwindled to being agnostic and receiving reward for being a good person as he put it. My heart was always connected to God and Islam. Nonetheless my sisters and I went on a girl's trip to Miami. There I was exposed to people places and things that I had never been exposed to at 33, that I had never been exposed to in adolescence and in my early 20's when the average person starts discovering who they are. I missed some of these steps because I lived an innocent life as a young Muslim woman there were just certain things Muslim girls and women didn't do. So, I was "Jane come lately to the party". While in Miami I did the real life, Julia Roberts "Eat, Pray, Love" thing and ordered things from the menu to relearn what I liked on my palette. The part where she talked about "marvel at something" I knew what she meant I went to museums and looked at the art, walked along the beach and let the hot sand penetrate my skin, I felt the mist from the ocean on my face seemingly for the first time. I was tapping into what I truly enjoyed. (I would spend the next 5 years going to the beach every chance I got just to recreate that feeling) The beach is my forever home and sidebar when Oprah calls and I make it big (another sidebar, kudos to you Oprah for being the symbol people use to confirm they've arrived)I will have a home on the beach! One with glass all around to let the light in during the day, a remote controlled blind system at night (I'm still a little afraid of the things that go bump in the night). That overlooks the ocean, so I can watch every beautiful sunrise and sunset overlooking the beautiful blue ocean as far as the eyes can see. (My little taste of heaven here on earth) Inshallah, God willing.

Miami was the first time I got a glimpse at God, but I

did not attribute what was happening to Him. I was still very much attached to the world, the four walls of my life, I still needed to mature, heal and grow in faith. So, it never dawned on me to pray or have gratitude for the moments I was experiencing. Life was still happening by accident, not purposeful, nor fulfilling in anyway. I came back from that trip refreshed and rejuvenated and ready to take on "my world" (Yes, I was still in selfish mode) I had this new-found energy and zest that would push me the next few months. I was always in this state of huge excitement and then this drowning feeling, there was something still missing.

In this constant state of chaos and worry. Always trying to control every situation and manipulate the outcome. Still in this place of ignorance and arrogance that I somehow controlled everything. Again, this false sense of how The Universe and God works. I literally paid to have people around me. I looked for people to help. The more destitute and needy the better, never realizing that all the drama I experienced was "by invitation". I was keeping myself in this hopeless, uncontrolled place by choice. I have only come to this realization this year and I'm still in awe of how much I was responsible for the pain in my own life. I was bent on blaming it on God though, not once in 20 years did I ever have a conversation with Him or seek to understand what was going on with me.

Shortly after the Miami trip, I marveled at God's

magnificent views on a cruise with my children to the Bahamas, I went to sleep on the ocean looking out to the moon over the seemingly unending dark water. When I woke in the morning, I rose to the most beautiful turquoise blue water that was so clear it appeared as if you could see all the way to the bottom. I forgot about being prone to motion sickness and I felt the warmth of the sun on my skin and it was then that I began to feel that there was more to this life than the misery and pain I had experienced. There was more to life than just working. I finally saw the smile on the faces of my children for the first time, in a very long time. I had been asleep this whole time. See I was in a domestic violence situation and I had stuffed my voice, my greatness down to fit in it. Every relationship or situationship I was ever in I dumbed myself down to be in it. I gave up some amazing part of myself hoping that by not trying to overshadow the other person with my greatness that it would somehow give them a chance to come up, catch up with me and we would rise up together and skip off into the sunset. There was also the religion thing, they weren't on my level Islamically or religiously. I remember speaking to my ex-husband and him distinctly saying to me that you have this pull on you and I can never seem to penetrate it and he said, "You will leave me for Islam."

He was right. That saying I used earlier, I learned from Christianity "Not equally Yoked". What I love about this is it described every relationship in this case marriage I had ever been in. This is not to toot my own horn or to make me look better than anyone, but I was the more intelligent and the religiously sound one in every relationship. Saying it now sounds awful because who am I claiming to be self-righteous and Godly, when I was nowhere even close to God!

I take the time to share this backstory because if you can imagine a really large pot, for my Latina sisters reading this just imagine the large pot your mother or grandmother would use to make "Sancocho". I was that large pot, and the ingredients in this case life experiences kept being added to this large pot, each time a new painful experience was added the already boiling water rose. Eventually the contents of my life, in this instance soup would spill over into my life causing a catastrophic mess. Habitual declarations that one day I'll get back to my religion "Islam" when I'm older and let me see if my spouse will join me "fully" in the religion spoke my hearts desires, but I never acted on them. The life I was leading was not for me I just somehow kept leading it with no real direction. Some of you may be able to relate to this because you're living it now. I thought that if I kept travelling down the road I would somehow meet someone that would rescue me from myself, happen upon that thing that would direct me to the light, a U-turn on the road that would help me to right all the wrong turns. Onward I went.

Another year, another trip, Puerto Rico, life continued

much as it was living the single life and hanging out with friends travelling and doing things that single people do, still being a mom and working. When I went to Puerto Rico there was the shift, a country with so many vibrant colors and hues (Purple doors on bright yellow buildings, colorful dresses among the natives and tourists as we walked down the cobblestone streets in old San Juan, and the surprising sight of Jack fruit growing on a tree right outside our hotel room door, I couldn't help but acknowledge God's presence. There was also this pull on me that I couldn't explain, I started referring to God more in my conversations with friends, co-workers and with my children. I was going through a lot inside of me.

I was determined to add adventure and more experiences to my life in hopes of finding me. I rode my first Jet ski with the bestie in Puerto Rico. As I paid for the ride, got on the jet ski and then rode out into the open blue water despite not knowing how to swim and with only a life jacket separating and protecting me from drowning I wondered how this experience was going to enhance me! God forbid I fell off the back of that jetski which almost happened as my eager friend revved up the engine to the jet ski and took off with me holding on for dear life. As soon as the instructor finished telling us the rules, I started calling on God because I was scared out of my mind, I said every prayer of protection I could remember. I trusted my bestie more than I trusted that life jacket or the jetski and even God at this point despite my prayers. I asked her "You do know I don't know how to swim?" I even asked her "What would you do if I fell off?" She reassured me she would come back for me. Thinking back on that experience I probably should have asked her all these questions before we left the safe confines of the shore. So I held on to her for the 30 minute ride out onto the open water. It was the most exhilarating and life altering experience I've ever had!

Back on the shore I laughed and struggled to catch my breath and then we had lunch (the best personal pan pizza I ever had, reminded me of one of Julia Roberts slices of pizza in Eat Pray Love) and pondered over my near-death experience. That night back at the hotel all I could think of was the reality of that situation, and I began to ask myself these questions. If something had happened to me on that Jet ski would I have been satisfied with my life as it was? Would I have given my children everything that they would need to get through this life? Would I be satisfied with my contribution to the world? Then that got me to thinking about my life, how had a benefitted myself and others? What was my contribution? What was my legacy? What was I teaching my children? What was happening to me? I would go another year growing and expanding my mind. One of the premises I started to live my life by was "Begin with the end in mind", Stephen Covey where he challenges us to think about the day of our death (much like Islam asks of its believers) what would you want people to say about you and how you lived your life. So, I started there.

This time I really started to put in the work, God in his infinite wisdom met me where I was. I was stuck, full of negative energy, with blinders and a thick seal over my heart. Bitter is a big word and I wasn't quite there but I was angry at life and hated the hand I was dealt. One thing I knew was I didn't want to leave this earth not having mastered myself, not having given myself a chance, leaving without living full out! So, I began the work!

The first thing I changed was my diet I cut out meat and I was never big on soda, but I lowered my juice intake. "Whole Foods" became my second home, as I browsed the aisles no one seemed to be in a hurry. It was perfect, so I slowed my pace, coming from a Native New Yorker this is almost unheard of, but I began to actually see the faces of people as I slowed my pace. I met a yoga instructor one day in the aisles, she struck up a conversation and she invited me to a class. I did not take her up on her offer, but it started me down the "Yogi" path, being universally conscious of my output and taking a minimalistic approach to consumption. I invited my 2 girlfriends using a Groupon to attend an outdoor yoga event and I was hooked. I found a quaint yoga studio just across the bridge in Bala Cynwyd just outside Philadelphia (who knew I would move into that neighborhood 2 years later) and started taking classes 2-3 days a week.

It offered everything I needed to grow, community, a calming environment (I always felt rested after every class) and a no judgement zone (Anyone that has ever been around Yogi's, knows that it's this eclectic mix of people from all walks of life that are brought together by different experiences usually those requiring deep, inner soul-searching work). Most people are not a fan of Bikram yoga, but I swear by it. I lost 12lbs in the first 2 months and my body started to tone. The days I didn't attend yoga, I meditated 15 minutes after I woke up. I started reading motivational books and my mind expanded. Most of the books touched on spirituality and I slowly started the internal conversation about religion. I remember talking to one of my girlfriends who is a devout christian about it. She was going through her own spiritual struggle at the time. Her advice "pick up your religious book." I wasn't ready, I knew the power of My Faith and I knew that as soon as I picked up "The Book" in this case, the Quran, the life I lead would be over as I knew it. I wasn't ready to walk into that unknown and face the very thing that had driven me from it in the first place.

Being the elephant in the room, because I rocked hijab. I hated walking into rooms or open conversations turned hushed voices, getting on trains and people moving to the other side of the train car, people rolling their eyes, I even had a broom thrown at me once. I just wanted people to see me and love me for who I was, not what I rocked on my head or how long my dress was or what their perceived perceptions of what I believed were.

Another year, yes, another year passed, and you guessed it another vacation this time I was off to Ixtapa, Mexico with one of my other girlfriends. We partied in Florida for her earth anniversary and then we flew to Mexico, she planned a fun yet relaxing trip. We planned horseback riding, mountain climbing, and cave diving and she asked what I wanted, and I asked about a yoga retreat. Well God again showed up because our villa was right next door to the "Present Moments: Yoga Retreat" check the name, how fitting right? I know! The town we stayed in is called Troncones and it was filled with Americans who had come to vacation years prior and never left! (I almost didn't come back myself, my children saved you all, if not you wouldn't be reading this book)

A quaint town, tucked away between the Sierra Madre del Sur Mountains and the Pacific Ocean. The day we arrived in Mexico it was sunny and beautiful, the closer we got to our villa which was about 45 minutes inland the more dismal and gray the sky became. It looked like the sky was going to burst. Even the driver was amazed by the weather as he said it almost never rains at that time of the year. We arrived at the villa still no rain just a full gray sky. Our driver dropped us off and we were met by the villa attendant, I want to say his name was Juan, he took our bags and gave us the key to our 2-story villa. It was truly something out of a dream, to date it is the last time I have been on vacation out of the country, which is strange for someone who travelled every year at least once, since as far back as I can remember.

I know there is a method to God's plan, so I don't complain. We followed him down the beautiful winding path past the other 2 story villas, when we finally stopped our villa was one of two that sat front facing the ocean just 100 feet from the foot of the Pacific Ocean. The scene was breathtaking, but not in the way you would think. We were both drawn to the ocean despite how threatening it looked. We saw gray water as far as the eyes could see. 1000 feet away, the water was raging, Tsunami like rage. We both exchanged looks like I hope this wasn't a mistake. My girlfriend left to unpack, I stood there. I was stuck, in awe of how the water was contained despite it splashing violently about. I knew there was only one force that could be responsible for this, God. He was there, I had travelled 2700 miles to come face to face with God. I just kept looking at the gray water and the heather gray sky. At one point the water started to creep along the shore, once it splashed my feet I awoke from my trance, became conscious of my surroundings, I remember what I can now describe as my inner voice saying, "It's Time", I knew exactly what the voice meant it was only once I heard that voice that

I moved from that perch.

Our first night was uneventful as the weather was not going to cooperate with us wandering too far from the villa. The other amazing thing about this vacation and this town was the limited access to wifi. There were truly no distractions, Wi-fi access was limited to specific times of the day and we literally had enough time to check in with my kids and post a social media update and then as quickly as we were connected, or should I say disconnected we were connected back to the *Present Moment*. That night I slept well but I was aware of the raging ocean the entire night. It's as if God was expressing his concerns and his commands for my life. I rose early the next day and expressed gratitude for Him waking me for the first time in years.

Alhamdullillah hil lathee Ayanna badama amatana wa ilaihin nashur (Praise is to Allah, God who gives us life after, He has caused us to die and to Him is our return) I did not perform the ritual style Islamic prayer (salat) but I did express my gratitude. I showered and went to the 1st yoga class offered at the retreat, 7am. Despite sharing the villa with my girlfriend, we slept in separate rooms and had different sleeping habits. I have always been an early riser and a "Grandma" at bedtime ready for bed at 9:30pm or 10pm. The first yoga class was even better than Bikram Yoga at Home, no rooms turned up to 100 degrees, we were naturally baked by the sun's rays by the time the class ended. The yoga room was out doors with a bamboo style awning that let ALL of the sunlight in. I loved it and I welcomed the cool mist from the ocean, yes that's how close we were to the ocean. I enjoyed the different instructors throughout the day and for the remainder of the trip. On the next to last day one of the teachers rested a cool washcloth on my head that smelled of lavender infused with other aromas, as she had done every class. For some reason this day I was crying uncontrollably the whole class, I had felt this deep connection to myself and God. I had felt the wind on the tip of my hair, my nose, my fingers, my back and even on my toes.

At the start of class I had this kink in my back that had been there for months despite my monthly massage package at a well-known hand massage franchise. At the end the kink was gone and so was the lump in my throat. I knew I was never going to be the same after this. My girlfriend who was not into yoga didn't get it, but she obliged me just the same, side eye included, I didn't mind. In between all this yoga were other amazing experiences that forced me outside of my comfort zone, Hot springs left the skin smooth, mountain climbing pushed me past my fear of heights on horseback and we came face to face with an extremely large bull. I felt no fear atop my horse "Guerrero" which means "fighter" how fitting, my son always says this about me, you are a fighter Mom, no matter what life presents you with you overcome it. I now know that has only been by the grace and mercy of God that I have been able to come through my life's most difficult situations. One of the final tests of my spirit and drive for what I now know would be the beginning of my faith walk was climbing this mountain. I thought we were going to ride horseback the entire way up and somehow despite my fear of heights (check the life metaphor/parable) I was resolved to that.

We dismounted the horses and tied them and proceeded to walk the other 500 feet, despite the 12lb loss my upper body was out of shape and I had no control over my breathing. Bad combo for mountain climbing as we went higher the air became thinner and I kept having to stop. My friend and the 3 guides called out to me to keep coming, I yelled "I can't", I'm tired" and "this is too much" alternating between retorts, every step of the way. Something I hear my clients say every day in my coaching business and I just yell back "Keep going you can do it". I'm so grateful to God for that moment. It was then that I developed the resolve to give this life ALL of me and to reach for greater within and outside of myself.

Finally, at the top I reconnected with my breath instantly and looked down and couldn't believe that I had done something that just 30 minutes before I said I wouldn't and couldn't. Then the treat was diving down the 300-foot drop into the Majahua cave filled with bats, bat droppings, stalagmites and stalactites, an unforgettable site. The ascent, descent and ascent combo were later symbolic, I had climbed out of the depths of my old life into my new life.

After that trip I looked for answers in books reading several in 3 months, listening to Youtube videos and struggling to return to my previous life with friends and at work. I went into a mild depression trying to figure out what was missing. The day I died to my old self is forever etched in my mind Thursday, August 27, 2015. I sat in an executive meeting at work with 100 of my peers, at lunch time, despite not eating I was nauseous and my face became extremely hot. I tried to return to my seat and I couldn't I felt like the world and the walls were closing in on me. I picked up my pen and my notebook and left and I never returned. I went to Friday prayer services(Jummah) the next day and so began the Awakening my return Home.

What was the pivotal shift for you? Think it hasn’t happened yet? You wouldn't have picked up this book if it hadn’t. Write it here

___

___

___

___

___

___

___

___

___

___

___

___

___

___

___

___

___

___

___

___

Step 2:

PRAY YOUR WAY OUT

I kept up with yoga and meditation throughout the process of coming out of my depression. I lost both of my best girlfriends through this transition within a month of one another they both found jobs in other cities and moved away. I know this was a part of God's Divine Plan. He can't do His work in you while you're distracted by outside noise and temptations from your old life. As a Muslim, prayer (salat) is one of the pillars of Islam and as I recommitted myself to the religion I became very aware of prayer time and made sure I prayed every prayer at its prescribed time. Despite having learned to recite the quran in arabic as a pre-teen and teen, I couldn't recall a single surah or ayat of the Quran, equivalent to psalms and verses in the bible. I remembered bits and pieces here and there, shame and disappointment in myself contributed to the difficulty I experienced over the next 3 weeks. I called out of work for 3 days and on the 3rd day I knew that this was something that was going to need some time and attention.

This was deeper than I thought. I got a full checkup and found out I had high blood pressure and other health issues that would require an even stricter diet, or they would get worse. My doctor asked me all my symptoms and the more she asked, the more she knew it wasn't just physical, she suggested I see a therapist. At first, I was opposed to the thought, this is unheard of with people of color and devout religious people. I contacted the EAP (Employee Assistance Program) through my employer and they sent me a list of providers. My therapist was the first name I saw on the list of over 100 providers. I did not bother writing down any of the other numbers, I dialed the number, she answered, her voice so sweet and inviting yet stern and businesslike. She reminded me of my grandmother who passed away 20 years prior. She had an opening that week and was eager to see me. I went to that appointment and at first, I spent the initial time convincing her, I was ok. Inside I felt closed off from the world and unsure. I had always been so confident, assertive and sure footed.

I never felt so vulnerable and exposed and what I had left I was working on protecting. She finally said, "It seems like you have it all together, what made you come here?" I lost it! The tears flowed, you ever cry so hard no tears come out and the middle of your forehead gets this burning sensation? It felt like my head was going to burst, and I let out a sob. I was tired, tired of holding it together and putting on the brave face that everything was ok when it wasn't. I had been doing it since I was 6 years old.

Now at 37, I wasn't ok, I was a confused, unfulfilled,

angry mess. There was no going back, if I was going to live my best life I had to let go of the secrets, they were holding me back and keeping me stuck, trapped in my own mind and body. I told her every story, I found myself wanting to catch the words as they left my mouth but as each word left I became noticeably lighter. I always thought of my grandmother during these sessions and how proud of me she would have been (if you recall, she is the best friend I talked about earlier in this book)

As I prayed more, God took more steps towards me and as I re embraced my beloved religion and way of life God brought me people to remind me He was present and to keep going. As it turns out my therapist's son was Muslim so when I used certain terminology that was related to Islam she was able to follow along which was extremely comforting.

Subsequent sessions she pushed me to dig deeper, push further to pull out the hurt and pain that I had pushed down. She had me keep a journal about my feelings towards my past hurts as the child version of Halimah. I would take care of my children's needs during the day and at night I would write out my deepest darkest feelings and emotions. It was extremely uncomfortable admitting some of the things to myself and then having to read them out aloud at the sessions. I'm forever grateful for having gone through this process, I faced my fears head on much like I did climbing that mountain top in Mexico.

As I regurgitated my past experiences I re-lived them in that moment which brought up a lot of the pain I felt when I was going through the molestation and the domestic abuse. The most amazing part was the prayer, when the terrible emotions would stir up it would be time for prayer. There were a few days in that 3 weeks that I dropped my daughter off at school and I would go back to bed only waking for prayer, there was one day that I missed picking up my daughter at the bus stop because I couldn't move I was so depressed. I performed prayer lying in bed it was all the motion I could muster. When my daughter used the spare key to unlock the front door and the door alarm triggered I somehow unlocked from the state I was in.

Determined to unlock my hidden truths, I took a leave of absence and went weekly to therapy on my own dime after that, I knew I needed it. I talked out my past and she helped me make sense of it all. I wrote my desires, my fears, my inadequacies and I prayed, I prayed every prayer and prayed in between those prayers. I finally was able to recall 15 surahs that I had previously memorized. The true test of my devotion came when I was able to pick up the Quran and read from it in Arabic. I was reconnected to His word and invigorated with His presence in my life. I was attending Friday prayer services on a consistent basis and surrounding myself with other Muslim women. For the first time I wasn't hiding, I never openly exposed my 20-year hiatus from Islam but when people asked I told them I had struggled. The more I admitted this to myself the better I felt. In my previous life devoid of God, I was a perfectionist, and everything had to be "just so."

The more I embraced Islam the less obsessed I became with being a perfectionist with worldly things. I wanted to do things that were pleasing to God. The more I did this the stronger and more confident I became. The whole time I was out of work on an unpaid leave and was living off my savings, my lifestyle was not cheap. Three months had gone by and I had to make a decision as to whether I was going back to work or not. Despite not having a job or anything lined up I decided that going back to my current job with the amazing perks and salary no longer fit into who I was and definitely wouldn't align religiously for me. This wasn't a simple, email your resignation letter and I could walk away, I had to return my company electronics. I left my company 3 months earlier as Halima with no H at the end, when I mentor the girls I always mention the significance, the world only knew a portion of me I left the extra "H" as what I kept hidden from the world which was my religious affiliation and the "HD" (high definition) version of myself. That day "Halimah" walked into headquarters in full hijab with resignation letter and electronics in hand. I was free. The life that I had created for myself was dismantled and over.

All my life I had been living someone else's life, living the lie afraid, concerning myself with other people's feelings. In the wrong hands it's a gift and a curse. I didn't know how I was supposed to use this gift of being an Empath. I always took the side of putting on my cape and working to help people solve their problems, because I knew what they felt, I had lived it. What I should have been concerned with was being a listening ear and directing them to discover their own healing. I wouldn't have birthed my children or my business if I had discovered this early in the game. Everything I've experienced was written and needed to go that way in order for me to develop as the extraordinary, dynamic woman I am today.

As a small child I was very aware of the emotional climate in my immediate surroundings. I learned to be a chameleon, adapt to the environment, smile even in the toughest of situations. What made my childhood bearable was prayer and the firm belief that somehow someday I was going to be out of this situation living a truly amazing life. God has afforded me some amazing experiences and I have truly lived a full life. Which is why I wrote this book. I wanted to share that amidst all the turmoil and pain there were many bright spots. I travelled and met some amazing people. They have all helped me to see God clearer. I sit in awe of Him at times at all the things He has seen me through. That although I have been scarred, he has allowed the wounds to heal. I couldn't see the miracles until I did the work (prayer) and gave Him the praise even in times of hardship. For God not only tests us with trials but he tests us with bounty. It's easy to seek God's face in times of tribulation and adversity but do you run to him with the same fervor in times of plenty and Greatness? That is the true test. Prayer is the key in the morning and the lock at night to this amazing life. Dennis Kimbro said, "Life is 10% what happens to us and 90% how we react to it."

As a kid growing up in a Muslim country, Medina, Saudi Arabia to be exact something I would later take for granted, prayer was a part of everyday life. Our life was planned around prayer instead of the other way around. My older (step) sister (I have an older blood sister too, the reason for making the distinction) went to school for the 3 ½ years while we lived there, and she went to school in the morning and was home by noon prayer. Shops and businesses shut down during prayer times. Everyone was either in their homes or filled the masjid for prayer it was the perfect situation for such a regimented religion as Islam. Something that is only hard to adhere to coming back to it after a long hiatus, if I had stayed the path I'm sure I wouldn't notice it. I look back on our time in Medina with very fond memories, on my journey back to Islam I can smell the crisp Medina air anytime I'm praying outside. The smells of the cleaning solution they used on the floors in the Muharram, fills my nostrils every now and then. When I spoke to my mother about writing this book she chuckled at the fact that I remembered the smell.

God somehow preserved these wonderful memories to be able to cling to when the days got rough. The hardest part of this journey has been the day to day activities, likening it to a time when my mind was swift, and memorization came easy. Recently I had a conversation with a spiritual coach and her words to me "Is it important for you to memorize the Quran because you want to relearn everything you knew prior to your hiatus?" and I told her "No" what's most important is that I'm able to read and understand the words so when I recite them they have more meaning. This resolve has strengthened my desire to learn and understand more, not boast about all that I have memorized. It's like children taking standardized testing, the goal should not be what level they have reached in something, but have they truly learned and retained the information.

Including prayer as the 2nd Step was essential, we pray first with our minds, tongues, and ultimately our actions. Many of us run from this step, as I told you earlier I didn't pray before because I knew my life would change. Hypocrisy and Faith, Faith and Fear they can't live in the same body, mind or heart it's one or the other!!! In those first three weeks of my transition from faithless to faithful I went through every emotion!!! I thought my heart was going to burst, I could feel my PULSE, my heart raced, it ached, and it loved!!! I prayed for FORGIVENESS, Prayed for CLARITY to understand my past everything I had been through I wanted to understand. I wanted to know the reason ALL these things that most people would have lost it over, happened to me!

God now had my attention, I prayed for DISCERNMENT, I asked God to show me what lessons I needed to learn from the past and to move forward into the future. It would be amazing to tell you it came flooding in all at once, but it didn't. As it took 20 years to create this life, it was going to take some time to unravel it. I'm so happy where I am now in my life, When I smile my soul smiles, when I laugh my soul laughs. I don't concern myself with what others think of me. I'm out of the box that I naively created for myself. Thinking that by stuffing down my strength, my voice and my religion. Keeping pieces of me hidden from the world that I was somehow going to be content living in this created reality.

If I could go back, I would tell 17-year-old Halimah "Don't do it Girl! She had no idea what she was doing to herself. So instead I write these words to you the reader "17-year-old {insert your name here}" this book is for you. I wouldn't wish those 20 years on my worst enemy, I have hurt myself and others along the way. I couldn't give them all of me, because I hadn't given birth to it for myself. Fast forward, it's one of the many reasons I created my company "Be You In HD, LLC", empowering women and girls to be their absolute best selves! I want to come out of these pages and hug you and tell you, "You are Enough". Preemptively I have said a prayer for every reader it goes a little something like this "I prayed for you to pick up this book, I prayed for you to read the pages with an open mind and an open heart, I pray that as the tears flow you let go of the life unlived, I pray you embrace everything that is possible for your life, I pray that you start saying "No" to who and what doesn't serve you, I pray you say "Yes" to God and yes to you" Faith without works is dead, If you want to take control of your life pray about it and then go to work to get it". Ameen!!! I wanted a relationship with God, so I had to stop talking about and be about it!

Being about it, is easier said than done but possible nonetheless. The day I prayed in bed sits in my frontal lobe like it was yesterday, I was fighting for my life laying there, fighting for the life I have now, I had to die to the old life, the old way of thinking, the old people that I had in my life, everything that embraced my old life. God sent them ALL away, so I could come face to face with myself and HIM! I am forever thankful for that day in Ixtapa, Mexico for God allowing me to see Him, I don't know how much more of that life I could take, and God knew it would be more than I could bear. As I'm writing these lines I'm holding back tears remembering the emptiness and pain. God All the while calling me, "Halimah prayer is the wifi, just connect to it, I promise you it goes all the way up." Prayer is how we stay alive, it's the daily preventative medicine we take, we up the dosage when we succumb to life's illnesses (doubt, worry, shame). Prayer is the life source, the air we breathe, whether you make dua, dhikr or recite the rosary call on God's name throughout the day. God promises for every servant who cries out "Oh Allah, I reply I am near." This is one of my favorite verses in the Quran, on those days when I need reassurance that although I don't see family, friends or the tangible results of my efforts, seeking God will help me manifest better relationships with family, new friends in faith and increased livelihood in all sense of the word.

No matter your religion here's a little homework for you:

1-Pick up your religious book of choice, Write your book here:

____

____

____

____

____

____

____

____

2-Open it up to any page, Write the Chapter, Verse or Scripture that you read here:

____

____

____

____

____

____

____

____

3-Over the next week work to incorporate it into your life! Write one word daily How it made you feel

Day One

____

____

____

____

____

Day Two

____

____

____

____

____

Day Three

____

____

____

____

____

Day Four

Day Five

Day Six

Day Seven

STEP 3:

PURIFY: YOUR SOUL IS YEARNING

My soul couldn't take one more moment of the "LIE", I had buried Halimah and lived as Halima for too long!!! I had travelled to all these places around the world, lived on or travelled to 5 of the 7 continents and as my mother always reminded me of the song "I've Never Been to Me" by Randy Crawford I had never been to me, never truly given my voice a chance to spill out, my own emotion, my own ideas and sentiments to roll across my tongue. I was always held captive inside by allowing someone, anyone's voice to overshadow mine.

Aware of my own intelligence, and letting just enough peek out as not to appear too brainless, just enough to fit in the circle. Living the lie, an outwardly full life and the truth, an inward self-imposed Hell. On occasion I would let out bursts of the magic and wonderment that was going on, on the inside only to be met with surprise as the genius within was not my familiar face. All of this self-sabotaging behavior in hopes that I would receive approval from people. My knowledge of self was skewed, I had not yet discovered that there was a greater purpose for my life. That in God's divinity, every circumstance was a setup for what He would have me take on as my purpose and the reason for my creation and rough upbringing.

DIVINE ORDER

In my experience, God wants us to follow his divine order and our soul has already been instilled with that desire long before we ever make it to this realm. That blissful place, in the pool of souls and then as breath is breathed into the bodies that contain our souls. God? I must confess that I always looked for you, I always chased and followed after you (I always thought I was running from you, but I was running from people and things that didn't serve me looking for you). I always knew you were there, I couldn't see you, couldn't place your face. I thought I found you in the sea of faces that crossed my path. I wanted them to be you and, so I placed more emphasis on them, I placed more love in my heart for the creation that I could physically grasp. The people places and things that were right in front of me in hopes of finding you.

If I only knew and fully understood love (حب) and Rahma (رحمة), I would have stopped looking for you in all the wrong places. Both of these forces are far greater than the love and mercy that comes from creation to creation. Love and mercy from creator to the creation, is a love stronger than that of a mother for a child. Almost unfathomable to me that God loves me more than I could love my children, as I love them with everything I am. (Able to feel their breath, their heart break, their sadness, their love, joy and laughter and wanting to remove the negative and barrage them with the positive.) I would have had patience and been content with where you had me in this life at every interval. While it may seem I'm regretful I am not, each of us on the path to God reaches Him via a different vehicle or avenue. God has an uncanny way of calling us to the path sometimes directly and other times indirectly.

Grateful for knowing what it's like to want for nothing as an adult, especially gratifying for a kid who went to sleep without eating sometimes, or eating leftovers until there was nothing left over, not having the latest style shoes, sneakers or designer jeans growing up. In His wisdom He gave me a taste of good things in this life, showcasing what was available and giving me reprieve from the tumultuous childhood I had grown accustomed to.

While God gives us the good, He wants us to stay in gratitude to Him, and not get distracted by the 4 walls of this life. I'm reminded of this anonymous quote "Don't trade your Akhirah for the Dunya" which stems from these warning verses in the Quran:

"Rivalry in worldly increase distracts you (from the remembrance of Allah), till you come to the graves" 102: 1-2

"Your wealth and your children are but a trial, and

Allah has with Him a great reward." 64:15

Muslims, followers of Islam, believe in the following phases of life Akhirah (The Hereafter,heaven) which is the final phase, Dunya is the first and refers to the period between life and death (The time you're in the world) and the middle phase Barzakh (is the period in the grave where you spend time waiting to be resurrected). I take time to explain this to anyone of faith that believes we were put on this earth to worship and praise God for creating this life and us. Our main concern is not the things we can attain in this life our only concerns should be attaining God's pleasure and striving for the infinite Good He has for us (Jannah, Heaven). Does He want us to suffer through this life? "No", but we were created to worship Him and should work towards this goal and be a reminder for those around us with our actions.

Name 5 actions you can take to start a prayer regimen

1____

2____

3____

4____

5____

What is your prayer Regimen?

Make a copy of this page and mark down each day you have completed your prayer regimen for the next 30 days. Renew this process every 30 days to stay on track.

Day 1 ____

____

Day 2 ____

____

Day 3 ____

____

Day 4 ____

____

Day 5 ____

____

Day 6 ____

____

Day 7 ____

____

Day 8 ____

____

Day 9 ______________________________________

____

Day 10 ______________________________________

____

Day 11 ______________________________________

____

Day 12 ______________________________________

____

Day 13 ______________________________________

____

Day 14 ______________________________________

____

Day 15 ______________________________________

____

Day 16 ______________________________________

____

Day 17 ______________________________________

____

Day 18 ____

____

Day 19 ____

____

Day 20 ____

____

Day 21 ____

____

Day 22 ____

____

Day 23 ____

____

Day 24 ____

____

Day 25 ____

____

Day 26 ____

____

Day 27 ____________________________________

____

Day 28 ____________________________________

____

Day 29 ____________________________________

____

Day 30 ____________________________________

____

STEP 4:

Love What Comes

I left one corporate job only to go into another, follow me the reason is symbolic, I was going to have to keep learning the same lessons over and over again. Lessons in humility, lessons in faith in God, belief in myself and conviction in my own abilities. What was truly important in this life was not attached to my job, my house, my children or any of the other material gifts God blessed me with. It has everything to do with me, as it relates to God. I would have to keep running back to homebase, God with every new venture, thought and action.

Full faith in God is a blessing not a birthright, constantly seek God to be bestowed this gift over and over again. Sinning or erring is a reminder that you're only human, do whatever it takes to find God's face, difficulty and adversity means you're headed in the right direction. Love yourself enough to speak up and go get what you want. The things God denied you require you to be patient not for what is better but for the time when you're ready for it!

I left the first job thinking that God wanted me to leave the first job because it wasn't good for my religion. I wasn't operating in full faith in God at this point yet. So, to keep me encouraged and on the path I resigned from a position that would have been too demanding on my time to keep me focused on my prayer. The 3-month leave afforded me my first thoughts of starting my dream business, helping to empower women of faith to live their best lives. With no real plans for the new position, I was back to square one within a year and inevitably I was so uncomfortable personally and spiritually that I resigned. By then I had developed my faith muscle and put the wheels in motion for my new business, I was ready to love whatever was to come.

Become so convicted in God and yourself that you entrust your past hurts and failures to give way to your present triumphs and future accomplishments. Begin to love that life the good and the bad. The fact that you woke up today, we woke up today is an affirmation that what God has for us is true, it's the chance to become more of who you were created to be and to move towards what you were created to do. Bouncing from job to job taught me the same lesson that going to college at 16 and 17 was supposed to teach me. Being in a new place where there were no other Muslims, teaching me how to navigate outside the familiar and safe harbor of the Muslim community. It was supposed to teach me to adhere to my faith in the face of adversity, to hold onto my faith in face of the taunts and jeers, to hold onto my faith when I didn't get the grade I wanted and when there were no places of refuge for prayer or reflection.

Adding this story and reflection in the "Love What Comes" Step was particularly important, when you can see God in the adversity or the hardship you will hold onto your faith. See faith is not something you achieve or a final destination or a lesson you learn and then never forget. Faith is an anecdote, as you become ill or sick from what life and the world throw at you, faith comes to cure it. Have you ever heard the term "New levels, New devils", well girl, as your faith increases so will the hardships! Faith is something that is ever evolving, it rises, and it falls, the test is to not quit. During the trials and tribulations, love what comes anyway, love and trust that God will send you only that which is good, even if it doesn't seem that way at the time. Let God magnify your understanding of Him and ultimately you, true faith comes from mastering self. Mastering yourself is about being truly honest with who you are and who you are not.

To receive the magnification, let go of the clutter in your life, of the people who have hurt you and this does not mean that you banish them forever but let the hurt and the pain that they caused out of your heart. Find love in the mundane, in the small things, it's enjoying and loving the small things that the big things will come. Start smiling, show your teeth, my aunt told me to stop smiling with my mouth closed, to show my teeth. I didn't understand what she meant at first when you smile with your mouth open when you laugh and your head tilts back you're laughing from your heart you're laughing from your soul. The more you love yourself, the more you love God the more you love people and the more you do to seek to be under God's grace and mercy. The more content and fulfilled your life will become. Love every situation good or bad, you never know which one is the one that will turn things around in your favor.

I'm so in love with this step, it's freeing and non-constrictive, you are afforded the ability to see things as they are not as you distort them to be. For 20 years I have seen the adverse of faith, disbelief I have seen what it can do to the heart, I saw what it can do to a life and I don't want to go back there, I don't want to perish as a non-believer of Islam never having loved God and myself fully.

All of the amazing stories of my past good or bad were ways for me to come closer to God. Every inadvertent act or purposeful sin brings you back to God looking for forgiveness and help, relief of that pressure in your chest. God's hold on our hearts, as the owner and sustainer of it, I had to go back to the beginning to appreciate what once was, let go of it, to take hold of the present and give way to the future. Affirm and love what will come thank God for what was, what is and what will be. Find the way up and out there's beauty in the struggle!

My Greatest take away from this step "Love what Comes" Is best expressed by a quote from Paulo

Coelho "When you want something all the universe conspires to help you achieve it". For a believer God is the owner of the universe and therefore when we pray, we know that God is already working on what we prayed for. When a servant asks a thing of God, God is shy to not give it to His servant.

To Love What Comes means seeing the world and people and things for exactly what it is. Not trying to put your own expectations your own inhibitions your own fears on that thing and on those people. My mother always used to say it's like trying to fit a square peg into a round hole it's not going to fit. Quit trying to conform situations and change people to fit how you want them to be. Love each circumstance for what it is and each person for exactly who they are. This may mean leaving situations and people that no longer fit who and where you are. God allows U-turns, don't be afraid to turn around and come back.

When I first came back to Islam after my 20-year hiatus even Surah Fatiha was hard for me, I couldn't remember what all the words translated from Arabic to English meant. Surah Fatiha, is the opening of the Quran, or the very first Surah in the Quran, it's also the key to open the heart to let God's love in. It is the reason it is recited in every prayer at the beginning of every rakat (unit of prayer), it's the mother of the Quran, the cure for the diseases of the heart. I recommend you start studying the Quran or your religious book of choice during this step.

I can read your mind, the first thing that you're asking yourself here is how difficult is this, it's just words on a page? As with anything when you're out of practice it's not that simple. Think about how difficult starting a new exercise regimen is the first 21 days. This is not for the weak, you'll have to put your ego and your pride aside. Days where you want to quit will come often, followed by mediocre days, where you don't want to go the extra mile. Do the work, it will be worth it. Those days give way to days where you will glide through and over obstacles.

In the holy Quran surah 50 verse 16 it is said that Allah is closer than your jugular vein all you have to do is reach out and call him. In this current climate and in this society people with faith will be looked down upon just as they were 1400 years ago. This Dunya, this world is a deception that is the trick of Satan, Shaitan or the devil however you choose to call him it is his trick to have us believe that this life is all there is that there's nothing more that there's nothing better. Well my veil has been lifted and I know that there is more out there I know that there's more for me in this life and that there's more for me in the next. God's help is near and, so I choose to seek his help.

His help is near, and it comes in many forms:

-Love directly from God, from a spouse, friend or family member;

-God's mercy

- Kindness from unexpected places

- A monetary contribution

-A traffic light turning green just as you turn the corner

- A stranger opening the door with a smile

- A kind word spoken

Many of us look for earth shattering signs of God's presence, His presence is in the everyday details. Come back to the shelter of God and all that is good. Ya Allah!

You're cooking with gas now, you should be experiencing some momentum by this step. Beginning to gain clarity be able to see the light at the end of the tunnel. Doubt is not welcome here. Stay the course. Some of you may have felt that you were too far gone to be accepted back into the folds of your faith. This is furthest from the truth, that stain that life put on you will always keep you in faith, it is a constant reminder of where you were and keeps you moving forward. Some may never experience a Prodigal life, they don't need the lesson to have faith. I was one of those people that needed the lesson. I pray me sharing my story keeps you from having to spend too much time learning the lesson.

Have you ever had a situation that you twisted and contorted to mean what you wanted it to mean? Write it here.

Take that same situation and ask yourself these questions

What really happened? (Ask others who may have been involved)

Was there something I did to contribute to it going well or badly?

Could I have done something to change the outcome?

What did I learn from it?

____
____
____
____
____
____
____
____
____
____
____
____
____
____
____
____
____
____
____
____
____
____
____
____

STEP 5:

Invest In You

Be careful with this step it's deceptive, this step involves self-care and most people think they are taking care of themselves when they go get their hair or nails done or partake in a little retail therapy. That's not self-care, those take care of the external, the superficial side of ourselves. Believe me a good massage and a facial and the new bomb "Ruby Woo" Red lipstick changed my whole perspective on life. But long after the massages and the lipstick have worn off what will I and you be left with? We will be left to the broken pieces and underdeveloped versions of ourselves. The more you know about yourself and ultimately God the firmer you stand in being all of who you truly are unapologetically.

How did I and how do you get there? I took time to work on me, the inner me. I took time to get to know myself first what I liked and didn't like. What truly made me feel some type of way, what made me happy and what I was unwilling to put up with in my relationships. The first thing I tackled was what I could control, ME. I turned off the TV when I came back from Ixtapa, Mexico I had gone a whole week without watching a news program or one of my fave TV shows, so I knew I could do it.

First reading books and articles about different things that I was interested in. Then seeking out places and events that aligned with those interests. Motivational and inspirational YouTube videos became a staple in the morning along with my morning affirmations. Beginning my mornings with 5 Affirmations, which quickly rose to the 20 I say to myself every day. As I grow and develop, I swap out an old affirmation, for one that suits the “new” version of me.

The importance of these affirmations is setting intention. The same way you set your intention to pray your prayers on time, to read from the Quran or your book of choice or to fast in sacrifice to becoming attuned to yourself. Set your intention for the day, the month, the year and ultimately for your life. You have the power to manifest things to come into your life. If you're at a dead-end job (dead end does not mean the benefits and perks aren’t great it just means you are not fulfilled and don’t see yourself doing this for forever) you can change your circumstances, make a plan and then work to achieve the job or business you choose to. A lot of people separate personal, business and career development I personally don’t believe you can separate them. Each of us is the sum total of every circumstance we have been through and found ourselves in. We ultimately make every type of decision based on all of those experiences. By taking care of your personal development, you will take care of every other aspect of your life. Choosing what you put in carefully, will determine what your output will be.

My next investment was in spiritual development, I advise you to take small steps here. It's like that first calculus class you take, so much information thrown at you at once and if you put your head down for a second to take a breather you miss a crucial step. Take your time here, this is not a competition, your spiritual development just like anything you do for yourself is just for you! Ask for clarification from a trusted spiritual leader and less from friends. While friends and even family may mean well everyone has their own interpretation of what something means. In my own understanding of the Quran everything is clearly written its people's own understanding and interpretation that brings about the questions and sometimes misunderstandings.

This book is entitled "Not Without My Hijab", so whoever is reading the book may experience it differently. I chose this title because my life revolves around my religion, the God of my own understanding. Islam speaks to me, to my heart and is the way I connect to God. The word Hijab loosely translated means "to cover", in essence my relationship with God is my covering. This means a Muslim woman wears hijab, a Muslim man wears hijab, a Jewish woman wears hijab, a Christian woman wears hijab. Any person who has a relationship with their deity whichever name they choose to call on him by wears hijab. There are many different interpretations in Islam, amongst Muslims about which is proper hijab,

I'm not here to tell you if there is a wrong or right way, just wanted to point out that the way you choose it for yourself is for you and to wear it proudly.

The goal of hijab is to show your allegiance to God, to be recognized and known. The physical manifestations of Hijab are the pieces of cloth Muslim, Jewish or Christian women wear on their heads the non-revealing clothing, a cross a Christian may wear around their neck. Their identifiers, they communicate to the world your affiliation just like wearing name brand clothes lets the world know which designer you like. What an amazing simile right? God is the ultimate designer, The fashioner, The shaper Al- Mussawir (one of the 99 beautiful names Allah calls himself by) and those who prescribe to the ideology of a deity know that we were put here to worship Him and to make his works manifest. Never let that desire to learn and develop in your faith die, keep the account open for deposits and withdrawals.

During classes and workshops the ongoing joke is that Islam is the religion for me. As a woman with beautiful and long natural hair a large portion of the time I spent in hiatus was wrapped up in something to do with my hair. Covering my hair remedies, me getting wrapped up in the superficial qualities, and takes away the need for comparison. Do the inner work, it will be the day it will start to matter less and less what you show the world and be more about your contribution to it.

As a recovering bragger, perfectionist and procrastinator, Islam is the perfect religion for me. The less I show the world the more the essence and true me comes out. All of the barriers have been removed. People are not looking at my outward appearance they can now see right through to my heart. They can hear the desires of my heart because everything else has been toned down and my insecurities are no longer screaming "Look at me".

Make continual progress in both your personal and spiritual development. Invest in your relationship with God and in the people, you decide to surround yourself. If you want to know how good of a human being someone is, ask those people that are closest to them. As a result of my troubled childhood, I didn't trust people because I hadn't forgiven myself and put my full trust in God. I kept people at bay, suffering from abandonment and trust issues because of the abuse and trauma. I gave just enough because I knew I needed people, I wanted to be loved, but loved on my terms. I would give people just enough of me to keep them interested and around me but just little enough that they knew they were temporary and that there was a piece of me they couldn't have.

Living my life in Hijab and in Faith I have worked to retrain myself, change my thoughts and ultimately change those self-defeating, self-destructive habits. I have loved many times but never truly been "in love" with anyone but once, never given any of my relationships a real chance, I never could give them all of me. The piece that was missing was the love for God and myself.

I spent a long time, 7 years to be exact alone, concentrating on work, my kids and friends never hoping for a new relationship. Chalking it up to maybe I'm just not meant to be with anyone. The more I learn about faith and Islam for myself is the more that I see that God created us in pairs, read the story of Noah's Ark and you'll get it. He created us together to help one another, to reproduce and to assist one another in worship. When one spouse is under attack by the enemy the other spouse can carry the weight of reminding and steering the other spouse back on track and vice versa. Don't be in a rush to find that person, the person God created to fill this space is made specifically for you. If you are harried in your decision you may fill the space with someone who has some but not all of the qualities. Even more so, I'm reminded of a recent conversation with a friend and he said, if you want a husband with the 80+ qualities you have written, you have to first become the wife that is worthy of that type of husband. Girl, that sentence was real, but I get it and this is true for every type of relationship. You want a great friend, be one, you want an amazing sibling, be one, daughter, be one.

God's plan has multiple strategies all to keep us focused on Him, to keep us focused on our worship and to help us achieve the ultimate prize Jannah (paradise). Some days I sit and reflect on all the things God has done in my life and I'm in complete Awe, I can't count how many times God has given me the answer to the test he put before me. His goal is not for us to fail, His goal is for us to pass. Our open enemy Shaitan, Lucifer or Satan has made it known that his goal is to take as many souls with him to the hellfire. God gives us choice, free range because He is certain that we will choose Him. He offers us hope and forgiveness at every turn waiting for us to choose Him. Think of a video game, if you don't pass a level it's not the end of the game, you can go back as many times as you want and start the level from the beginning and try and try and try again, until you master that level. Does this sound familiar? Yes, it sounds a lot like God, He keeps giving you the same lesson over and over until you pass until you "get it"

The way to manifest the things you want in your life is to charge up the batteries and keep adding new information (like apps on your iPhone, the phone has amazing features but can do miraculous things once you add the apps). At this step don't get a new phone looking to start over, make full use of the phone you have.

The people you have in your life should be audited at this point. Who can stay? Who needs to go? And what level of attention will you pay them at this point. Nurture the relationships with your family and the people who support you.

Write a list of 3-5 people that are a positive influence in your life and that you desire to take on this journey (next 6 months to 1 year)

1-______________________________

2-______________________________

3-______________________________

4-______________________________

5-______________________________

In one word describe your relationship with each person:

1-______________________________

2-______________________________

3-______________________________

4-______________________________

5-______________________________

Develop a 3-step plan for each person on how you are going to repair and nurture the relationship. Examples: Set-up a lunch date; A day to call each person and follow up; Repeat these steps as needed to continue to nurture the relationships

Person 1:

____

Step:1_______________

Step:2_______________

Step:3_______________

Person 2:

____

Step:1_______________

Step:2_______________

Step:3_______________

Person 3:

____

Step:1_______________

Step:2_______________

Step:3_______________

Person 4:

____

Step:1_______________

Step:2_______________

Step:3_______________

Person 5:

____

Step:1_______________________

Step:2_______________________

Step:3_______________________

STEP 6:

Change your Heart

"Only from the heart can you touch the sky.' It is only through purification and cleansing of the heart can you first cure yourself, reach others and ultimately find God. Don't know if you thought you could skip past "Forgiveness" as a step, but I'm here to tell you that you can't! Forgiveness is an arm of self-care and faith. Start by forgiving the person in the mirror. Forgive yourself for not wanting to forgive those that hurt you. Forgiving your perpetrators or your transgressors releases the hold they have on you. Releases the grip that the circumstance or situation has on your heart. I have had many a day where I stopped remembering to breathe while I had a flashback of being molested, of being thrown down a flight of stairs, of having yelled at someone who had done nothing to me. I became so engrossed and captivated by the memory and had somehow teleported back to that time and space and allowed myself to feel those feelings and emotions and immediately started to feel that emotion in the present. Sometimes becoming angry at myself for not having fought back, advocated for myself or for being too aggressive.

Therapy taught me to feel the emotions and not suppress them, the anger, the betrayal and the sadness. Going back to Step 4: "Love What Comes", let the emotions wash over you instead of internalizing them, forgiveness allows you to experience that moment in the present and immediately go towards forgiveness. Start with yourself first, forgiving yourself and recognize that you are not in that space, nor are you that person anymore and the circumstance no longer has power over you.

I forgave myself for not speaking up, for not doing more to help others find their way out, for not screaming or crying out the first time I was violated. Spiritually speaking forgiveness allows you the ability to pray for someone who once harmed you, there's redemption in that, there's love and mercy in that. Praying for a past transgressor will give way to God forgiving you for yelling at someone in traffic, for taking your bad day out on your spouse and other major and minor sins you may have committed. The mercy you show others will result in God showing mercy towards you! One of the greatest things I have learned on this journey has been changing my heart. It has also been the hardest. When my therapist had me reach out to my molester, I didn't hesitate, I wanted what was on the other side of that, "closure" and healing. I wanted to know the what if, his reaction to my words "I forgive you". Part of me prayed for an apology and the other part of me prepared for his denial and dismissal of the incident. So, I tracked down his number and found a quiet space (only after God prompting through hearing a Quranic verse with the person's name and then someone mentioning the person's name a couple of days later) and I called the person.

In God's infinite wisdom he orchestrated the scene perfectly, softening my heart and the heart of the person. I cut to the chase and explained the reason for my call. The person's reaction was the total opposite of what I expected. I was prepared to have the person deny that it happened and to be arrogant about it. Instead he apologized for what he had done, and even thanked me for being so merciful and kind. The closure I was looking for was to be vindicated and have the upper hand. God instead gave me compassion for the person, made my heart softer and I prayed for the person that whatever sickness(es) he endured as a result of what he had done that God cure him of them. I've spoken to the person a few more times since and each time it has helped a little more. I'll be honest if I never speak to the person again I'm whole and complete and healed but the desire for the person to pay for what they did and the anger I once had is gone. I can no longer be hurt by this person without my permission and God has made it so that his life has been a series of trial after trial. While we as victims/survivors are searching for justice God is taking care of the Punishment.

There are more people to forgive and even more people I have to seek forgiveness from. I start with myself first. Everyday expressing my love for myself, for the choices good and bad that I have made and thanking myself for continuing to move forward in spite of the obstacles. It's easy to quit, it's easy to say I'm doing great for an orphan, doing great for having survived molestation and domestic violence and abuse twice, doing great for having failed relationship after relationship. I don't want to be doing great in spite of those things, I'm doing great because those things happened to me. I'm doing great because I choose to look to God for the answers, I choose to talk to Him about all my problems. I choose to follow what my heart and my soul want regardless as to how many times my heart has been broken or disappointed.

I think about Thomas Edison and the creator of the light bulb, they failed thousands of times and eventually got it right. I'd rather keep working on changing my heart getting it right, than to not try and stay where I am. Never truly knowing how great I could be and how close to God I could become.

In the past 2 years, I've relearned a bunch of Short Surah's and studied their meanings and purpose and worked on applying each of them to my life. The benefit has been that it has softened my heart and it has showed me to be less rugged with people. More accepting of them for who they are. It's still hard accepting that some family and friends are not on the new path with me. I want for my brother what I want for myself, I have found so much happiness and peace on my current path and I want to share it. Your spiritual enlightenment, is just that yours. We have to come to it on our own, there's no help or urging you can give to someone who's not ready. The best thing you can do for yourself is to let them go, let them find their way to the path. Be an example, show them what the enlightened path looks like. If and when they're ready your paths may cross again. The worst thing you can do is to try to bring them along, carry their weight and choose when this is for them. Notice the title of this book it's "Not Without My Hijab" not "Not Without Your Hijab" Reclaiming your Faith is a personal journey that you take alone and only when you're ready! So, don't expect "old people" (friends and family) to join in on your enthusiasm along the road. God will send "new people" to embrace you at every step of the way and even if He doesn't, know that you embrace you, you can celebrate you and that God ultimately acknowledges and accepts you for you.

Changing your heart is about accepting the new you, gaining clarity of who you are at each new level, healing the wounds from the past, forgiving and loving people and giving generously. Be grateful for everything that God has blessed you with.

Are you holding a grudge against someone? What is the grudge? Explain.

Do you need closure? How will you attain closure?

What was the result if any?

STEP 7:

Activate Your Faith

Get ready to add Faith back into your life! I spent 3 months in seclusion. Building up my faith muscle to be able to face the world. Islam much like Judaism is a difficult religion to practice in today's modern times. Especially for women in a world where everything is sexualized, and we are all desensitized. It's one of the reasons my hijab came off in college in the first place. I didn't think I would be taken seriously and that I would be overlooked because the first thing they would see was my hijab instead of "Hey she's amazing" Learning to love the hijab wearing image that stared back at me, God had to show me what the experience was like living the total opposite of my upbringing and foundation. In order for me to grow and have an appreciation for it, it wasn't enough to be born Muslim, I needed to grow to understand "Why I was Muslim?" Why I chose the faith? I needed to strengthen in my faith, build a firm foundation for when the "World" would inevitably bombard me with questions about "Why was I now donning this headwrap? Had I changed? Was everything ok? Was I being forced to wear it? and so on.

I had to be comfortable with me in my renewed faith before I could present it to the world.

Affirming your faith is key here, it's less about you telling other people and more about being convicted yourself. I explored other religions Christianity and Buddhism and studied Judaism briefly. Growing up Muslim it was the only religion I knew. I didn't study the other religions growing up. Something I would strongly suggest to parents now. Exploring other cultures and religions with your children is not teaching them to love the others but allowing them to see why they love their own. Develop a religious plan much like you would plan out your business or career path. What will you study? Who will you study with? Who will you teach what you learn? Who will hold you accountable?

It helps to have a plan and a support system. Too often I see women who take on a new faith and they fail. They fail because there's no plan and it's not implemented in phases it's everything at once. This is idealistic but not realistic. Human beings are weak, we succumb to our wants and desires more often than we refrain from them. Even more so in this "Microwave generation" where everything is "Now". Finding people that I could call or text to talk me off the ledge and hold me accountable to what I said was paramount. None of these people were Muslim by the way. They loved me enough to know that I was serious, and they listened and championed my efforts. Once I became concrete in my decision I was able to move in to phase two which was still not covering, but praying.

Consistent in prayer I looked to surround myself with people that believed as I did. I went to the mosque and started building relationships with other people. I activated my faith by affirming my allegiance to Islam publicly. The day I became convicted was the day my hijab went from a cute side turban, to a longer version similar to the one I wear today. This happened quickly for me because I was ready, I was born Muslim and therefore knew what I was getting into.

For new shahadas I don't suggest this, get attune with who you are first, I see a lot of women go from wearing nothing over their head to full abayas only to come out of it in 6 months sometimes sooner. Wearing Hijab no matter the religion carries with it a certain responsibility not to be taken lightly. It's like someone who starts a new business you have to be fully committed in order for it to work. In my coaching I suggest people try new ventures on a part-time basis before they dive in. I feel the same for faith. Get to know what you're getting into before you take the full leap.

Once your faith is activated, you know this is the path you want to choose, set deadlines for yourself. Set-up time to study your religion or book of choice. Set dates when you would like to be finished learning a particular Surah or chapter. Gain clarity of your understanding from your trusted religious leader, then find someone to teach it to.

For thousands of years, people have known that the best way to understand a concept is to explain it or teach it to someone else. As we teach a particular topic we learn ourselves. This will ensure you do your due diligence to learn the subject yourself. I don't know about you, but I don't want the responsibility that comes from misinformation. What results is an endless cycle of people that will work to improve what they learn. The real beauty comes when the student becomes the teacher and the teacher becomes the student.

Again, faith is not an achievement it is confidence in what we believe and what we anticipate will happen as a result of having it. Faith gives you the assurance of manifestation of and from things you cannot see. Faith is a muscle; it needs to be activated by us and then strengthened through exercise by us. Faith is not a natural ability we are born with, it's a trait gifted by God and then learned. Much like we learn or commit scriptures to memory.

Activating faith does not mean you'll have a life devoid of obstacles, it gives you a foundation, a guide to refer back to when you meet adversity. A means to find your way back if you veer from the path. The greatest benefits from all the stories and obstacles I have shared in this book, is that it has enabled me to develop my faith. Each obstacle is an opportunity for us to trust and believe in God more. Faith is about how we respond to God and what He tests us with.

Faith is about trusting that what God has for you is

best. Affirming and renewing your affirmations to God daily. Praising Him for the good and the bad. Being grateful for the opportunity to experience the good and the bad.

Affirmations are extremely important here, prayers are affirmations expressing what we desire for our lives and for ourselves. Full belief in God, that He has already bestowed on you the life you desire, you just have to go get it!

Here is an affirmation poem that I wrote one morning after Fajr (The Dawn Prayer):

Relentless

Relentless oppressively constant, incessant, persistent, continuing, constant, continual, continuous, non-stop, never-ending, unabating, interminable, incessant, unceasing, endless, unending, unremitting, unrelenting, unrelieved; I AM RELENTLESS!

I will not be outworked

People don't understand how the accolades keep coming,

I AM RELENTLESS

I serve a God who is unrelenting,

He opens the floodgates of abundance and everything amazing

For His servants that give Him all the praise

That sacrifice food, sleep, comfort and luxury

I am relentless in prayer in the third of the night while others lay in their bed sleeping

I am relentless before dawn (Fajr) I awake and stand in prayer unrelentingly praying without ceasing

Looking for a little bit of Favor from the king of kings,

The lord of lords, THE ALMIGHTY, *oh what a wonderful God I serve*

I will not be outworked!

Despite the obstacles, the barriers, the difficulties I AM RELENTLESS

Don't try to outwork in the physical what is being worked out in the supernatural and the spiritual

You ask me "How I do it?" the more important question is "Why?"

My prayer every morning and five times a day is that my life be about service to others

That my time here on earth not be wasted

That my next deed be better than my last,

That I may earn the favor of my lord;

You ask me how I'm so successful on this side of heaven?

I am relentlessly seeking the things you cannot see

I am seeking the view of trees as far as the eye can see, a view beneath where rivers flow, a view that no human eye has seen

I have my sights on a bigger prize, so please stop asking me "How I do it" and ask me "Why?"

Because God is, I AM RELENTLESS

I recorded this affirmation poem and posted it on my social media pages this year as a declaration of my faith, tangible evidence of my "Why?" and a way for me to hold myself accountable to my goal. Anytime I have an off day and wonder why I'm doing all of this I play this poem. I am a slave of Allah and therefore everything that I am and ever hope to be is owed to Allah, so when my ego gets the best of me and I somehow believe that I am responsible for willing something into existence, I remember that only because God Is, I am.

What affirmations have you enacted in your life?

____
____
____
____
____
____
____
____
____
____
____
____
____
____
____
____

Example of My Affirmations of Faith

1- Daily I have a better relationship with God

2- I will inspire 5 people today to embrace God

3- I will read the word of God today

4- I am successful by the will of God

5- I pray for my brother/sister what I pray for myself

Week 1: Write 5 Affirmations and recite them daily

1- ____

____

____

____

____

2- ____

____

____

____

____

3- ____

____

____

____

____

4- ____

____

____

____

____

5- ____

____

____

____

____

____

Week 2: Write 5 More Affirmations and recite them daily

6- ____

7- ____

8- ____

9- ____

10- ____

Week 3: Write 5 More Affirmations and recite them daily

11- ____

12- ____

13- ____

14- ____

15- ____

Week 4: Write 5 More Affirmations and recite them daily

16- ____

____

____

____

____

17- ____

____

____

____

____

18- ____

____

____

____

____

19- ____

____

____

____

____

20- ____

____

____

____

____

____

STEP 8:

Trust God and Trust Yourself

(Amana)

Guilty! This feeling will overtake you if you let it! I spent a good portion of my time and effort in this step. It took me forever to get over the fact that I was talking from both sides of my mouth. Saying that I loved God and Islam but spent 20 years not adhering to the faith. Many people of faith look at us, the prodigal children as devoid of feelings, empathy, sympathy, regret, remorse and guilt. As a believer and person of faith, this couldn't be further from the truth. As I read the Quran anew, I learned so much that I didn't know. Things that were pretty basic as a Muslim. Finding renewal in the way I made wudu(ablution for prayer). The way I was reading a few surahs was incorrect. Some of my ideas about hijab changed, Surah Nisaa Verse 60, I learned that older women do not have to don the hijab if they are past marrying age. How beneficent and merciful is Allah. Again Islam presents choice to its followers, God entrusts us with ourselves as to how we govern the practice of Islam in daily life.

Amana in arabic loosely translated means fulfilling or upholding trusts. Al-Amanah, The Trust is the moral responsibility of fulfilling one's obligation to Allah(God). Meaning followers of Islam or any religion are willing participants, willing servants. Where guilt lies is we often misuse the trust, ignorant to the magnitude of the consequences. The first time I took off my hijab at 17, I never thought it would be 20 years before I put it back on. Which is why this is a self-help book, I cautionary tale to the young and a guide for the mature or young at heart.

Born and raised into the Muslim belief system, I should have known better. That this world will suck you in and have you believing and doing things, that are far from your values and morals. The Quran clearly states that we are strangers, not meant to fit in this world and not to partake of it. I fell as many of us have fallen, broke the trust, my covenant with God. Those are the internal and external demons (nafs) I fight every single day to not fall into those same self-destructive, lazy patterns, I use the word lazy because religion takes work when it's easier not to practice, why would you want to?

Hey Girl, speaking to the adolescent religious reader here, don't trade places with me. There are no words to truly describe what I have done to myself, I may never be able to communicate that to you. I'm not God to tell you what has been recorded in my book for me. When I talk to God in prayer I'm easily brought to tears, out of guilt and shame. Hope in God's forgiveness keeps me going, He shows me in many ways that I'm on the right path. When I do works that are in line with the life He has chosen for me and He rewards me with Good. I spoke earlier about faith being a gift, not everyone will be given this gift. There are those that are entrusted with upholding it for themselves and using their platforms, voices and gifts to have others see God through them.

The Amana speaks to your commitment to God, your relationship with Him, the world would have you believe that adhering to these customs from a religion that was introduced over 1400 years ago is absurd. In fact the opposite is true, in the 3 years since I have returned to active faith, life has become easier, my heart lighter and I have a greater sense of peace. No longer quick to anger, road rage gone, mindful of my speech, ever cognizant of what my hijab represents.

Before I put on my hijab I first made the intention to do so, sure my intention was pure. Asking God to direct my steps and to give me the strength I would need to observe hijab. Strengthening the other manifestations of faith, I started with the Quran and Salat (praying) 1st with 1 salat a day, then 2 and then all 5. Ensuring that I was making my prayers within the prescribed time and then at the prescribed time stopping all activities and work to pray.

Muslims follow a lunar calendar so as the seasons change, the prayer time changes. These are the prayers in order:

Fajr -Made before Dawn

Dhuhr -Mid Day Prayer

Asr -Late Afternoon Prayer

Maghrib - Early Evening Prayer

Isha -Late Evening Prayer

There's a pretty popular app that most Muslims use to determine prayer time in their time zone or region called *Muslim Pro,* I have found it most helpful.

I started fasting non-obligatory days to increase my closeness to God and to reflect on my life, where I had been, where I was and where I was going. I started to rebuild my trust in and with God.

I thanked Him for everything He entrusted me with, my faith, my voice, my talent, my story, my sight, my limbs, my organs all were created for me to use in the way of my creator. My children are a trust, a gift from God to protect and raise them. As a woman who has experienced miscarriages, I know what it's like to not be able to have children, so I am grateful for the ones that I do have. The miscarriages were another lesson in trusting and loving God's plan for my life. He knew 4 kids and Halimah would not have worked.

Wealth, the type of work that you are given as a

profession is a trust. Allah too will test you with that, if you don't do the right thing with what is entrusted to you God will take it away. Until an appointed time where He will return it to you when you are worthy of it. (Reported by Al-Bukhari, Chapter of Taking Away the Trust, no. 6131)

What I have found most helpful in keeping with the trust is to check my intention with everything that I do. Am I doing this for the pleasure of God or to serve myself in some way and make the adjustment as needed. In writing this book I found it difficult at times to keep going. Was I writing this book to fulfill myself in some way or was I writing it to help others. I have read this book over hundred times before I submitted it to the editor for this reason. I wanted to ensure that this served the world, that women and girls were given empowerment tools and exercises to guide them back and keep them on the path. Avoiding the many pitfalls, I myself succumbed to.

What are some ways you can check your intention or regain focus when you fall off? Who will you check in with when this happens? Who will hold you accountable?

____
____
____
____
____
____
____
____
____
____
____
____
____
____
____
____
____
____
____
____
____
____
____
____
____

Step 9:

Inspire Others

Surrender yourself to God! Put your full trust and faith in Him and inspire others to do the same. Let go of the need and desire to need to know what's going to happen next. A lot of people say, "I hate surprises", every day you wake with breath in your body is a surprise! Life is not owed or promised to you. God is in control of you, your destiny, he owns your entrance, existence and your exit. The word Amana in arabic means fulfilling or upholding trusts. It is the moral responsibility for those who believe in Islam to fulfill one's obligations due to Allah and fulfilling one's obligations due to Allah's servants.

When you've been let down by people as often as I have it's easy to lose hope of having relationships you can depend on. The relationship with my grandmother was the only true relationship I had, and I even lied to her about being molested thinking I was protecting her from heartache when deep down I knew she already knew. Manifestations of the abandonment, showed up in failed friendships, marriages and familial relationships, I spent an inordinate amount of time invested in relationships where we were each codependent on the other. When I helped them out of their situations and they were able to stand or their own and no longer needed me, they left. I was disappointed and no longer useful. Through the attachments I put all my worth in them.

The people were not to blame. I was to blame. Looking for my self-worth, validation to come from an outside source, in all the wrong places you come up empty handed because you're looking for fulfillment in something that won't suffice you. Other humans are not equipped to handle all of our complexities. We are sent to one another to serve a purpose. Our goal here was always to seek the answers of our existence from the creator, to rely on him for our sustenance. Our nature is to want the best (hence the desire to be perfectionist) our souls were already in paradise and we know something better. Now inside these bodies and in this life, we are looking for that here instead of realizing that we have to work to get back home, to Jannah. That's my inspiration and what I work to help others see in themselves.

Hang tight to the rope of Allah. There's only one relationship that you can truly depend on and that's the relationship with God! He is everything, He is a healer, the All Knower, the Forgiving, the Compassionate. The same way we look for validation from others, we should look to seek God's validation and approval of our deeds. As long as we are following

His commandments we have His approval and Love. Even when we make mistakes He treats us with love.

I traveled the globe searching for fulfillment, the same fullness I have found in my living room praying on my plush, turquoise, white and yellow prayer rug. (It's one of my faves!) I use it when I'm traveling so it's been to quite a few places with me. I have shed many a tear, asked for forgiveness, for redemption, for a million-dollar business, to be able to help people out of their situations and for this book to help people to see God more clearly on that prayer rug! Some prayers have been granted, some delayed and some flat out denied, I'm not deterred because I put my full trust in God.

The miraculous journey back from my 20-year hiatus is what keeps me renewing my trust in God, the way He has placed me in rooms, on committees and on stages where my qualifications dictate I shouldn't be able to go. The mighty God I serve removes obstacles, people, lack of resources and circumstance. I bear witness that there is no God but Allah and Muhammad (saw) is His messenger (La Illaha illallah muhammadar rasulullah).

Many of us are quick to not trust God, I raise my hand because I've been guilty, but He has honored his servants and slaves by giving us each the choice to worship Him or not in Surah 13 Raad (The Thunder) vs

19-21

Allah has honored you by giving you reason; the ability to choose who and what to follow.

Trust in God's will and timing, He will leave you to yourself for a while and let you "live", YOLO (You Only Live Once). When you have gone too far and are in danger of losing your way, He brings you back. How do you know when it's time to "come home?" "Reclaim your Faith?"

If you are reading this book the time is, NOW. What are you waiting for? How much time has to be lost? There are many people living active and full lives and are still devout Muslims, Christians, Jews and the like. I have done more covered in Hijab than I did uncovered. Renewing your Faith does not mean you become an overnight "Islamic Scholar" or Nun. If you want my advice don't become that either, unless you want a quick way to lose all your friends and family and be sent into exile. Start with planning your day around daily prayers, then work to incorporate time for study with your religious book, attending weekly prayer service and whatever other activities you find increases your spiritual health.

How's this for inspiration, You are invited to Islam; An

invitation that is extended and answered during each of the 5 daily prayers. You proclaim your faith at least once in every prayer. You choose Islam and then keep choosing it during each prayer. Pay close attention to the words and really feel them in your heart.

Consciously follow in the way of Islam or your religion of choice, in upholding your duty and your agreement with Allah(God), eyes wide open, fully aware of your intention and the reward for your adherence and good deeds and the punishment for straying and your bad deeds.

Protect yourself with the words of Allah, (this one is still an adjustment for me) we get caught up in our mundane every day activities and often forget to read and feel the words of God. The days I pick up my holy book the Quran, revealed over 1400 years ago, the words jump from the pages describing an instance or instances that happened that day or week. His words are a reminder that although we plan He is the best of planners. Those that read are informed and have a responsibility to teach, inspire and empower others to do the same.

Deen or religion is to be observed everywhere you go,

your Faith should inform your life not the other way around. The services I offer in my company Be You In HD, LLC work to educate and empower women to be their best selves and live their best life as they incorporate their faith into their life. What I love about serving the Muslim woman is that our faith governs business as well and I don't have to hide that fact when conducting business. Look how different life looks now.

At 17, I thought the world had come to an end and that there was no space for me as a Muslimah Powerhouse in business if I did not assimilate. Excuse me as I clear my throat and ascend my soap box, if the reason you are removing your hijab or straying from your religion is to fit in because of a job, a relationship or for anything other than your own beliefs. "Stop, collaborate and listen." Don't remove your hijab, don't denounce your faith! Work to incorporate the Quran or your book of choice into your life and gain a better understanding of the reasons we wear hijab or have certain guidelines in your belief system. Get your life, or in this case religion so you can make more informed decisions.

God rooted me in my faith, Islam at a young age to prepare me for some of the pain I would endure while simultaneously saving me from the ills I would experience later in life. When I would become so arrogant, that I lacked empathy and that it would be returned to me reminding me of how merciful God has been to me over the years.

Problems in relationships stem from making that relationship more important than Him. He will cause you great emotional pain until you move away from it and towards the direction of Allah. It's not to say you can't love your spouse, your children or some of the other blessings in your life it's to say that that love can't be greater than that which you have for Allah!!! Speaking of which...pause break it's time for Dhuhr.

I'm back, by inspiring others you'll stay on the path. God knows the weaknesses of the individual. By working to inspire others who prescribe to the same faith deepens their faith or understanding and essentially strengthens your understanding and keeps you grounded. Keeps you from going astray. Remind others of the reason they were all created. Many Jehovah's Witnesses spend their days in an effort to call more people to The Kingdom a quality of their religion I admire.

Get grounded and confident in faith, you are a producer and an owner, meant to create from your own hands. Again, my recommendation is to schedule your prayer times, daily devotion times and then everything else. God first everything else is secondary. It is my prayer that this book and chapter has inspired you to have renewed faith in God and belief in yourself.

How will you get started? Ask yourself are you Spiritually disconnected? Do the people and things that you surround yourself match your faith?

What steps will you take to inspire others?

________________Here are some of mine

1- Temper the things that are your areas of weakness and opportunity;

2-Grow what will help you help you and help others

3- Daily make an investment in your akhirah (next life)

4- Acknowledge where you are and ask for forgiveness.

Prophet Muhammad (SAW) asked for forgiveness over 100 times a day as narrated by Aisha (RA)

Step 10:

Operate in Optimism

Staying positive and optimistic in your faith in a negative and cruel world is about being proactive and consistent. In the Northeast part of North America where I grew up and live we experience the difference of all 4 seasons. Each season bringing with it a positive and negative attribute. The same can be said of our current political and Islamophobic climate. We cannot control what other people say and feel, like we can't control the rain, the wind, a hurricane, tornado or blizzard. What we can control is how we react and conduct ourselves. The same way a soldier prepares for war a religious person prepares for people who will challenge or oppose your religious beliefs by studying and becoming more learned in the religion.

In elementary school when I would fast during the holy month of Ramadan, we would go to lunch and all the kids would ask us why Muslims can't eat. I would start explaining and then have to go into defense mode, because people would go into imposing their beliefs or understanding about what I had just explained to them. People would say "Well if fasting is about purification, you can still achieve that omitting things from your diet, allowing you to drink water or chew gum. The short answer is "No you can't!" It was those small nicks or cuts as Michelle Obama put it during her speech at the 2017 PA Conference for Women that became the reason for the shakes in the foundation at

17. I had become exhausted building up my confidence every day about something that I did not fully understand myself.

Recalling these experiences as an adolescent, lead me down the negative path and shook my religious foundation what seemed like small compromises lead to larger ones. Before I knew it, I was at the point of no return and life as a Muslimah was unrecognizable. It's up to you to turn the car around from going down the wrong one-way street. It's never too late, and my advice is to not wait for something major to happen or to be taken away from you before you return to God and remembrance of him. He prepares you for the trials and tribulations, comforts you through the hardship and sees you through.

The devil has a team, that has grown from negativity and hate, their whole role is to convince you not to pay attention to God to keep you in a state of disbelief, stuck. They will sometimes promise you wealth and riches whatever your heart's desire. You then become a slave to whatever that thing is, and you are in this constant loop. Wanting more of that thing, could be "money", "power", "love", "drugs" and any other vice. The best thing you can do is seek God for everything that you need and do. By doing this He will keep opening new doors when old doors close. He will leave you a trail of breadcrumbs to find the thing that He wants you to find. He will give you success in something that advances his kingdom or in a Muslim's case "UMMAH" and simultaneously benefits you in this life.

Love will conquer hate, evil and deception at every turn. It is up to you to build up your positivity and remain optimistic. To exude patience (sabr) and perseverance. Sabr is not just patience, it's taking action, taking action in your religion and persevere with the commandments even when everything around you is falling apart. To build up your love. Your bounce back muscle. A Lot of people ask me how I'm so positive all the time. What I am surpasses positivity, its optimism on 20 as they say. My faith teaches me to have "hope" in God's favor and blessings. To weather the storm, I'm reminded of a line from Mrs. Celie's character in "The Color Purple" when she says to Ms. Sophia "This side be over soon, heaven last always." While I don't believe in taking life lying down, I do believe we should ride this wave called life. Take the good with the bad, learn from the setbacks and mistakes. Don't waste your time on things that are outside of your control, pray for deliverance from those circumstances. Don't start over when you fail, start where you are.

Islamophobia and the current state of the world towards Muslims is not meant to wipe us out as a society or religion its meant to strengthen us. Its apparent in the number of Muslims in the world today 1.6 billion and counting and the 2nd largest religion in the world.

Negativity is all around us, we can find it when we turn on the news, when I walk down the street and people prejudge because of the way you're dressed or even the way the you look. At a recent Khutbah (Friday sermon for Muslims), the Imam talked about how our deeds will be measured on the day of judgement, God is not looking for how beautiful you appear on the outside but how beautiful you actually are on the inside. It's easy to default, defer and deflect responsibility to someone else instead of facing yourself and conquering you. I challenge you, the first person to overcome is you!

These days I operate in optimism and expectancy, my faith in God dictates that what I pray for and believe in God for I will receive. I don’t worry like I used to because of it. To say that worry has totally disappeared would be a fabricated tale, when I find myself doubting I reach for God, I call out to Him. Asking Him to renew my faith and restore my confidence.

You will reach for the "Renewed Faith Jar" often, don't be afraid or deterred or even ashamed. Many people ascertain that to renew your faith means that you'll never lose it again. Having faith is a lot like having a business or being a full-time entrepreneur depending on the time of day or circumstance you may have Quit. Don't! Keep reaching for God, get so grounded in His word you can recall the verses in your time of need or despair and recite them. Stay prayed up. It is the only way you'll survive the madness of the day.

Now I know your like, This is too hard! At first it will take work, just like anything the more you practice the easier it gets. The business that has been around 10 years has an easier time coming back from a setback than a business that has been around for one. Faith Muscle memory activates, and you spend less time searching for what you need to do in each circumstance. I'm looking forward to hearing your progress. Be sure to email me or connect with me on social media about your progress here. I know some days will be daunting but other days your connection to God will overwhelm you and you'll wonder why you waited so long to connect.

What are 5 things that you can do to remain optimistic in hard times?

1-____

2-____

3-____

4-____

5-____

Surround yourself with likeminded (positive), non-judgmental people. Name 5 people that you can call that will raise your spirits when you are down.

1-

____

2-____

3-____

4-____

5-____

Something I found particularly helpful was to have my favorite Positivity Quote written and posted strategically in places to keep me focused. Write your favorite quote here and post at your workstation, on the fridge and/or as a screensaver.

Step 11:

NEVER STOP SEEKING GOD

Finally, the last step, the act of making Tawbah seeking God and asking for forgiveness. For the sins committed knowingly and unknowingly. I would hope that your sins belong to the latter category, but I must raise my hand because I have knowingly committed sins as recent as this week that I'm writing this paragraph. What kept me away from my beloved God and religion so long was I stopped seeking forgiveness. I thought that I was too far gone for God to forgive me. I had lost hope in being forgiven and had conceded to a "damned life" for lack of a better word. God offers us hope in His redemption. As long as there is hope there is no such thing as a condemned man, I know serial killers, child molesters and Murderous leaders are up for debate.

I found the beauty of God as I began my ascent, to get closer to Allah's grace and majestic throne. I found amazing stories of defiance, hope, forgiveness and resilience in the Quran, like the story of Yunus(as) known as Jonah in the bible, when he was swallowed by the whale. Yunus went against God's ask and guidance, abandoned his mission and was thereafter punished and thrown into the sea, subsequently swallowed by the whale. I implore you to read the story for yourself but long story short, He stayed in the whale for an undetermined period and only after consistent prayer did God order the whale to surface and plant the prophet on an Island where He continued supplicating to God and asking for forgiveness. If this was the test of a prophet, what do you think of what we will be tested with. The lessons to be learned from this story can be summed up in

Surah 21 Al- Anbya, Ayat 87 And [mention] the man of the fish, when he went off in anger and thought that We would not decree [anything] upon him. And he called out within the darknesses, "There is no deity except You; exalted are You. Indeed, I have been of the wrongdoers."

Wow, how just and swift the punishment and the mercy. Which of the favors of your lord will you deny?

Continuing to seek God, is crucial to staying on the path. There is no sin God won't forgive if you ask for forgiveness sincerely from Him, He promises His Love and His mercy or Rahma. His Rahma is far deeper than His Wrath. Faith gives you shelter no matter what is going on in your life. Writing this book was my way of showing that you too have control over your destiny and can take back your life. Let go of the haphazard living and thinking, truly honor God and everything amazing about this life. I have sat bedside in hospitals and on deathbeds watched family and friends heal and others slip away into the next phase of life. Each travelling one step closer to God and what is destined for them from what their hands (actions) have wrought in this life. I pray for their safe journeys and for healing but never once envied them, grateful for the reminder (this could easily have been me) and for more time to truly master myself and grow from life's lessons, that God has been trying to show me all along.

Never stop seeking God, keep going back and focusing on the steps as needed. Ground yourself in your religion and know that "How you are with people, God will be with you." The most beloved actions and the easiest way to reward is to bring happiness to the heart of a Muslim(believer) and to solve the problem of another Muslim. True Islam is about service to others, being of benefit to the society where you live, work and raise your family. The 25 named prophets in the Quran came to serve who, the people! One of Prophet Muhammad's (saw) major lessons was to pray long and hard at night for your heart's desires for this world and the hereafter, so you can work to bring them into fruition and be of service during the day.

Maintaining your religious identity will be hard and arduous I'd be lying to you if I told you anything else. It's a lifelong process, there will be dips, curves and bends in the road. Allah will see you through them all if you rely on Him for everything in your existence. Those who adhere to the remembrance of God are referred to as "strangers" because people have long ago taken on the role of creator as opposed to "the creation", very different from being a consumer and a producer. A consumer is here to take, and a producer is here to give. I am honored to say I am God's creation, operating as a producer of what is in my capacity to produce and a stranger in this land and life.

Work hard to rectify your heart, ensure it is sound while you're on this side of life to gain a lofty position in the akhirah. The things that benefit us in this life, money, family and cars will not benefit us on the day of judgement nor in Jannah. As I stated earlier, the scales on the day of resurrection do not encompass the superficial like they do in the dunya. Do things in this life that will weigh heavy on the scales in the hereafter inshallah. Check your intention regularly when you give, pray and fast.

One of the many tools I use is the power of positive affirmations, the law of attraction in the form of Dhikr, Dua and beginning with the end in mind. Seeing things before you see them and operating in full belief that God, the universe will bring them to fruition. I see Heaven, nothing like it will really look like but I imagine myself there, I'm curious as to what God's face looks like and anxious to see the family and friends that have long since transitioned, as their faultless, beautiful selves.

Dua of Light (Nur)

One of my favorite Duas (prayers), the invocation for going into the masjid and one of Prophet Muhammad's (saw)supplications while in Sujood:

O Allah, place in my heart light, and in my ears light and in my sight light, and above me light, and below me light, and to my right light, and to my left light, and before me light and behind me light. Place in my soul light. Magnify for me light, and amplify for me light. Make for me light, and make me light. O Allah, grant me light, and place light in my nerves, and in my body light and in my blood light and in my hair light and in my skin light. [1]

O Allah, make for me a light in my grave...and a light in my bones. [2] Increase me in light, increase me in light, increase me in light. [3] Grant me light upon light. [4]

[1] Reported by Al-Bukhaari 11/116 (Hadith no.6316)

[2] At-Tirmidhi 5/483 (Hadith no. 3419)

[3] Al-Bukhaari in Al' Adaab Al-Mufrad (Hadith no.695)

[4] Al-Bukhaari Al-Asqalaani, FathulBaari 11/118

I'm reminded of Julia Roberts in Eat, Love Pray I'm a

woman in search of her word. A woman still finding her words, finding her voice. No longer chasing God but looking for the things that remind me of Him. That keep me in remembrance of Him. Leaving rooms where I don't feel His presence and saying "No" to projects with worldly gains, that go against my beliefs. As a firm believer in God I'm no longer running from the greatness of myself or letting judgement from other people deter me from greatness. Holding steadfast and firm that religion and God relationships are about choice, God presents opportunities (tests) for you to choose Him, despite the negative worldly consequence. I've been offered 6 figure salary positions that go against my religion, that I have been told to remove my hijab for to attain. While enticing, I declined, I can no longer push down who I am as a Muslim woman for the temporary pleasures of this world.

I've had friends say, "Girl I would have taken "XYZ" position and asked for forgiveness later. I have made compromise after compromise during my 20-year hiatus, when does the compromising end? At what point do I take ownership of my life? At what point do I put my trust in my creator that what He has destined for me will sustain and suffice me.

I'm often approached after my workshops, in gatherings and speeches where I share the same stories I shared in this book and I get asked. How was I able to come back? I get asked "Why are people so judgemental and more importantly "Why do I care?" The more I practice, the more I read about my beloved religion, the more I'm convinced that my 20-year Hiatus was a deflection, I was worried about what others thought, worried about trying to fit in a box. God never intended for me or us to fit in a box, He created each of us differently, He created different kingdoms, realms and beings with similarities but different. The common thread is we are under his hijab (covering) all working to be in a constant state of worship to Him.

Our accomplishments, religious adherence is a mirror reflection of the work we have put in. When your life and religion are on display for others to see, you become a reminder of a life unlived, choices unmade, accomplishments never achieved and a life devoid of a relationship with God. No one wants to be reminded of what they're not doing. That is not the plight of this book. I'm not forcing my way into homes looking to convert people. I'm looking to hold the hand and guide those that want to come willingly that need a little help to find their way.

Refer back to this book periodically, I suggest the last 2-3 days at the end of every month, at least for the first year. Think of this as spiritual exercise. The more you invest in your spiritual health, the more you will get out of it. Look back at it at the end of the year to see your progress. As a Muslim woman I wear my allegiance to my faith on my head, some wear it on their forehead (bindi, Hindus), others wear it around their necks (cross, Christians) and there are many other symbols around the world, I point this out because the more I learn about Islam the larger my hijab gets, and so as not to be misunderstood, Hijab is a symptom or symbol of what's going on on the inside which is why it has evolved from me not wearing it, to the turban side bun, to a loose fitting version of the one I wear now.

Keep moving forward in faith, when I hit negative patches I look for more information, attend Jummah, sometimes I switch masjids to keep myself from becoming complacent. Do what you have to do to stay connected.

The gist of what I'm saying is that the moment you stop seeking God is the moment you'll fall back into misery and chaos. Keep searching for God even on the days when you don't feel like it, on the days where you don't want to give it the effort. On the days where it's easier to walk down the street without hijab, so you can disappear into the landscape. Hijabi (Oh Covered One), You were meant to stand out! God knows us better than we know ourselves, why do you think He has us say "La Illaha Illallah" so many times during our salah throughout the day? He knows that our faith will waiver, as a full-time entrepreneur I liken this to how many times I want to quit and go back to working for someone when I have a low sales day. Just like in my business you will get over this feeling. You will come back to your senses and belief and be able to move forward. I'm so thankful for "The 11 Steps to Reclaiming Your Faith", I'm so much happier, living a more caring and productive life. I'm more excited about getting up in the morning even on the tough days where the list of "to do's" is long and bills are longer than my money.

Giving Gratitude to God is the first thing on my list every morning. I make the time to meditate, I schedule prayer time first and then plug in my appointments. Knowledge of the steps while critical, it is in the "A.P.P.L.I.C.A.T.I.O.N." of these steps that you will experience the true power that "Reclaiming Your Faith" affords. I've included a summary of the steps below:

Step 1: Awaken

Step 2: Pray Your Way Out

Step 3: Purify-Your Soul is Yearning

Step 4: Love What Comes

Step 5: Invest In You

Step 6: Change Your Heart

Step 7: Activate Your Faith

Step 8: Trust God and Trust Yourself

Step 9: Inspire Others

Step 10: Operate in Optimism

Step 11: Never Stop Seeking God

What are some daily activities you can commit to that will ensure you stay connected to God?

Record the days you complete each activity over the next 365 days by writing something you're thankful for that date.

I am in no way a religious scholar, nor do I have a degree in religion and I make no claims that I am the perfect servant or Muslim. I wake every day in gratitude to God, in awe of everything that He has made manifest in my life. Grateful for the path He has chosen for me. My path is riddled with obstacles but most of them are self-inflicted. What you believe will become your reality. So, choose wisely! I make no claims on how things will go minute by minute for you, but if you have picked up this book there is a desire to manifest something better in your life.

Faith for me is Islam, your path may be different, but what we have in common is the need to feel a deeper connection to God and ultimately ourselves. God is a master orchestrator if you allow Him to have His way in your life you will experience some pretty amazing things on this side of life. Be open to them. Love What comes!

Use the activities at the end of each Chapter to develop your Faith Plan using the 11 steps. Much like a business plan, developing your faith plan creates the roadmap for reclaiming your faith, gives you guidelines to refer back to when you go off course. As faith becomes the foundation to everything you do, be rest assured that once this plan is in place everything else will fall into place. I would love to hear your progress, be sure to email me at

halimah@beyouinhd.com

or connect with me on any of my social media sites

@beyouinhd

Made in the USA
Middletown, DE
22 June 2025